WHAT EVERY CHRISTIAN OUGHT TO KNOW

Basic Answers to Questions of the Faith

RICHARD S. TAYLOR

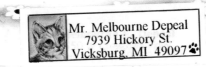
Beacon Hill Press of Kansas City
Kansas City, Missouri

Copyright 2002
By Beacon Hill Press of Kansas City

ISBN 083-411-920X

Printed in the
United States of America

Cover Design: Ted Ferguson

Library of Congress Cataloging-in-Publication-Data

Taylor, Richard Shelley, 1912-
  What every Christian ought to know / Richard S. Taylor.
    p. cm.
Includes bibliographical references.
  ISBN 0-8341-1920-X (pbk.)
  1. Christianity—Miscellanea. I. Title.
  BR96 .T39 2002
  230—dc21

2002000959

10   9   8   7   6   5   4   3   2   1

CONTENTS

FOREWORD

I first met Dr. Richard S. Taylor in the 1960s. He came to Scotland to preach at the historic Sharpe Memorial Church, Parkhead, Glasgow. Later he came to speak at a youth camp at Bowness-on-Windermere in England's Scenic Lake District.

What always impressed me was his clarity of mind. This professor of theology and missions from Nazarene Theological Seminary could speak with coherent logic. That was what we Scots really appreciated!

Dr. Taylor does not claim to be infallible nor to answer every question or say the last word on everything in this book. Indeed, if Dr. Taylor were teaching a class of graduate students as he did for so long, he would have much more to say and would go much more deeply into many points.

But this book is not written for theological specialists or graduate students. It is written as a thinking layperson's introduction to theology. It gets away from technical jargon and presents Christian truth with verve, clarity, and balanced common sense. I particularly appreciate the way he explains the connection between God's sovereignty and our God-given human freedom. Without that freedom we would be puppets. Only *with* that freedom could we enter into a relationship with God of genuine *personal* love. It is from this that Dr. Taylor develops his very helpful discussion of the doctrine of God's providence.

All of that makes this book a very practical discussion of theology. Dr. Taylor shows how an understanding of Christian doctrine helps Christians approach the spiritual questions we all face: How can I be forgiven? How does God guide the circumstances of my life? Does God send hardship and tragedy? What does it mean to be holy?

Most important of all, this book stands in the great tradition of central, classical Christian orthodoxy that C. S. Lewis called "mere Christianity." It does not wander off the path to the left—

into that "liberal" Christianity that was designed as an answer to "modern" doubts and is now fading away along with "modernity." Nor does it wander off the path to the right—into that fundamentalistic Calvinism first fully formulated as a logical system in the 17th century and still influential among many sincere Christians. Rather, here is a contemporary expression of that great central tradition of Christian doctrine shaped by the Christian fathers *before* Augustine—Irenaeus, Clement, Athanasius, and the Cappadocians—and described by Wesley as *truly* "catholic" (universal) Christianity. Here is one immensely experienced teacher's expression of genuinely Evangelical doctrine. I commend it most heartily to any reader who longs to inquire into the inner logic of faith.

—Thomas A. Noble
Professor of Theology
Nazarene Theological Seminary
Kansas City

PREFACE

The famous British playwright Dorothy Sayers said, "If we really want a Christian society, we must teach Christianity, and it is absolutely impossible to teach Christianity without teaching Christian dogma."[1]

"Dogma" is doctrine—the kind of doctrine that is not up for grabs. It is the kind declared in the creeds of the Church. Teaching dogma in the way Miss Sayers had in mind would require being *dogmatic*. Horrors! In everybody's mind these days, being dogmatic is not a virtue but a vice. Who wants a teacher who is dogmatic! Not many do—especially in this age of relativism and "postmodernity," when even the existence of Truth with a capital *T* is doubted.

But like it or not, this is exactly what Dorothy Sayers says is necessary if we would have a Christian society—or a truly biblical Church or an evangelism that accomplishes the Church's mission. For that matter, it takes dogma to save souls. This is exactly what Paul said to Timothy: "Watch your life and doctrine closely. Persevere in them, because if you do, you will save both yourself and your hearers" (1 Tim. 4:16).

But if teaching doctrine is the goal, there must be Christians willing to learn and some way to teach them. This book seeks to explain as clearly as possible some of the basic doctrines. The assumption is that these doctrines are so basic that the title of the book, *What Every Christian Ought to Know*, is entirely justified. Even the word "ought" has a dogmatic ring about it. But so be it. The firmness in the word "ought" can be defended:

• Knowing the basic truths of our faith is a matter of simple obedience. We are commanded to "be prepared to give an answer to everyone who asks" for the reason of our hope (1 Pet. 3:15).

• The Great Commandment says, "Love the Lord your God with all your heart and with all your soul and with all your mind and with all your strength" (Mark 12:30). Seventy-five percent compliance will not do! Yet many Christians are weak, porous, and ungrounded because they love God with everything but the mind. It is time they brought this part of themselves to the Cross also and discipline it into good stewardship. If they do, they will grapple with the basics that every Christian *ought* to know.

This book came close to being titled *Questions Thinking Christians Ask*. That would have been suitable also, for every Christian *should* be a thinking Christian, and thinking Christians *do* have questions. The aim of this book is to anticipate those questions—at least some of them—and try to answer them clearly, correctly, and biblically. That is why I am using (for the first time) a question-and-answer format.

Not all questions thinking Christians might raise will be answered in the following pages. I hope that the questions I am ascribing to my readers and attempting to answer at least "scratch" where my readers are "itching." And I sincerely hope they will stimulate further thinking and perhaps further questions. Other topics, just as basic, cry for treatment, but they will have to wait for another book. In the meanwhile a list of books "for further reading" given at the end will, I trust, prove helpful.

—Richard S. Taylor
Bremerton, Washington, 2000

THE BIBLE
Can You Give Me an
Overview of the Bible?

QUESTION: *What sort of a book is it?*

ANSWER: It is the Sacred Book of Christians. Actually it is a com-
pilation of 66 books, written over a period of some 1,500 years by
perhaps 40 authors. The volume is divided into two main divisions—the Old Testament and the New Testament. The Old has
in it 39 books, and the New has 27. It covers the subjects of God,
humankind, sin, and redemption. Its story unfolds within the lives
of the people called Israelites (Hebrews or Jews). The Bible traces
God's creation of this people as those called out with a distinctive
mission. That mission was to channel God's self-revelation to all
peoples and to provide the matrix for the coming of the Bible's
central Person, the Lord Jesus Christ.

The Bible was written originally in Hebrew and Greek. It
contains the following literary divisions: the Pentateuch (the first
five books), containing the account of creation, basic early history, the beginning of the Israelite nation, and the Mosaic Law;
the history books; a poetic and wisdom section; and finally the
Prophets. All of this is in the Old Testament. The New Testament consists of four Gospels, presenting the person and work of
Christ; the history of the Early Church, called the Acts of the
Apostles; and various pastoral letters and doctrinal treatises written by members of the apostolic circle. The final book is a
prophetic, highly symbolic kind of literature, the Revelation, or
the Apocalypse.

During the time of Christ, the Old Testament was the Bible
of the Jews, who used it every Sabbath as the basis for their study

and worship. The same book was used as God's Word by the Early Church. Gradually the writings of the apostles and their coworkers were added to the Old Testament as an additional basis of Christian worship and instruction and as constituting also the authoritative Word of God.[1]

QUESTION: *What is the Bible about?*

ANSWER: The answer has already been given: God, humankind, sin, and redemption. But to that answer we must add "with a focus on Jesus Christ." He is the Key that unlocks the whole of Scripture. If we do not interpret the Bible in the light of Christ, we misinterpret it—always. When two friends were walking on the road to Emmaus (according to Luke's account), they were trying to make sense of the recent events. Jesus had disappointed them by allowing himself to be crucified. Now even more puzzling was this fantastic rumor that He was alive. When Jesus joined them, incognito, He unraveled the mystery by explaining the Scriptures. First, He rebuked them for being so dull in their failure to understand "all that the prophets have spoken!" Then He proceeded to explain to them "what was said in all the Scriptures concerning himself" (Luke 24:13-27).

This clearly implies that while the Old Testament (their Bible) is about creation, humankind, sin, Abraham, Moses, the Israelites, and the prophets, all of this remains an enigma until resolved by the coming of God's Son, the Lord Jesus Christ. In Jesus we find the Scriptures' true meaning. Not creation, not humankind, not sin, not any of the other subjects, but Jesus is the Bible's focus.

QUESTION: *If Jesus is the focus, what is the purpose of the Bible?*

ANSWER: To show us the way to heaven and how to walk en route. Paul states this in utter clarity in his final letter. He reminds Timothy, "How from infancy you have known the holy Scriptures, which are able to make you wise for salvation through faith in Christ Jesus" (2 Tim. 3:15). There are two things here: First, the central genius of the Bible is its ability to make us wise for salvation. But second, the Bible makes us wise by pointing us to Jesus Christ, in whom we must put our faith.

QUESTION: *If the Old Testament could make Timothy "wise for salvation," what is the need for the New Testament?*

ANSWER: The Old Testament revealed a holy God, who loved humanity and was both merciful and just. It revealed the history of humankind in its creation, its assigned role, and its terrible rebellion. It revealed God's methods of dealing with humankind's rebellion and corruption and how God built bridges to people through His various agents, such as Noah, Abraham, and Moses. But throughout its record ran a persistent theme of redemption, the details of which pointed to a divine Redeemer. The classic description of this coming Redeemer was in Isa. 53. If the Jews had properly understood this passage, they would have likely seen that their Messiah must be a suffering Savior—providing redemption from sin—before being a universal Ruler.

Now to answer the main question: Why the need for the New Testament? Isa. 53 was prophecy, not history. The Messiah needed to come and fill out the blueprints provided in the Old Testament. Everything there pointed forward. The New Testament records the fulfillment. In the New Testament we have the arrival of Christ, the record of His teachings, the account of His death and resurrection, the worldwide spread of the Good News, and the apostolic interpretation of these momentous events. So we need the New Testament to understand more fully what the Old was able only partially to reveal, that is, the complete nature of this salvation that Paul was writing to Timothy about. "For the law was given through Moses; grace and truth came through Jesus Christ" (John 1:17).

The Law was like a garment pattern with very detailed specifications. But the pattern can't be worn. It will not protect anyone from the cold and wind. It must be turned into a wearable garment by grace and truth. Only Jesus can turn pattern into reality.

QUESTION: *How do we know that Jesus actually spoke the exact words ascribed to Him in the New Testament?*

ANSWER: We don't unless we can believe in at least one saying reported by John: "The Counselor, the Holy Spirit, whom the Father will send in my name, will teach you all things and will remind you of everything I have said to you" (John 14:26). If we are not sure Jesus even said this, then we are sure of nothing and may as well quit the ship right now. But if we can believe that in this statement John was demonstrating the fulfillment of Jesus' promise by quoting accurately, then we have reasonable ground for accepting as authentic all other sayings ascribed to Jesus.

According to the careful historian Luke, the promise of the Holy Spirit was actually fulfilled on the first Day of Pentecost after Christ's death and resurrection. At once the Holy Spirit began reviving the memories of the apostles exactly as Jesus had promised. Thus no sufficient reason exists to doubt the historicity of what they recorded, including the discourses of Jesus.

QUESTION: *What authority does the Bible have over me today?*

ANSWER: The authority of God. When Jesus rebuked the Jews for putting their traditions ahead of Scripture, He said, "Thus you nullify the word of God" (Mark 7:8-13). To read the Gospels is to become convinced that Jesus' thinking was totally governed by the assumption that the Scriptures were His Father's Word. "For Christ," writes Erwin W. Lutzer, "the words of Scripture were God's words. For Him to say, 'Have you not read?' is equivalent to saying, 'Do you not know what God has said?'"[2] To disbelieve the Scriptures therefore is to disbelieve God. To scorn the Scriptures is to scorn God. To disobey the Scriptures is to disobey God.

What the Bible teaches about right and wrong, about sin and salvation, is what God teaches. As Gerhard Maier comments, "There can just be no doubt that in Jesus' eyes the Holy Scriptures were accorded an incomparable authority. Anyone who finds 'criticism' of the Old Testament by Jesus must turn things upside down to do so."[3]

QUESTION: *What is the source of the Bible's authority?*

ANSWER: The inspiration of the Holy Spirit. Some have claimed that the source of the Bible's authority is the inner testimony of the Spirit to our spirit that God is speaking. Such a testimony exists, but that is not the *source* of the Bible's authority. It is rather the Spirit's *confirmation* of that authority. The authority lies in the action of the Holy Spirit in producing the Bible as a creation of His personal inspiring activity. Each individual book, when written, started out as a Word of God. There never was a time when it *became* a Word of God (or *becomes* a Word of God to me as I read it); it was God's Word at the moment of writing. Not only so, but also it is the authentic Word of God whether I personally have any inner witness of that fact or not.

This is what the Bible claims for itself. If we cannot trust the Bible's witness to itself, we have no reason to trust its witness about any other doctrine. "For prophecy never had its origin in the will of man," writes Peter, "but men spoke from God as they were carried along by the Holy Spirit" (2 Pet. 1:21). Clearly the controlling influence here was not the creativity of the writers but the action of the Holy Spirit. Paul declares the same thing: "All Scripture is God-breathed" (2 Tim. 3:16). This was not some kind of celestial remote control. God's relation to creating the Scriptures was like blowing His breath.[4]

QUESTION: *What is the scope of the Bible's authority?*

ANSWER: It covers everything we need to know for our salvation. We certainly need to know about God, creation, God's law, God's mode of action, the nature of sin, the person of Christ, the provision of Atonement, future destiny, and all such important matters.

QUESTION: *What was the Holy Spirit's mode of inspiration?*

ANSWER: It was a direct impression on the minds of the writers of such a nature as to ensure that what was written conveyed accurately the truth God wanted it to convey.

However, there are two extremes concerning the nature of inspiration to be avoided. One is an extreme form known as "dictation." This is the belief that the Spirit dictated every word in a way that made the writer little more than an automaton. This supposes that the writer did not need to investigate other sources or rely partially on previous records. The Spirit provided all the facts and words. The writer did not need to think and make selective judgments but only passively let the words flow, almost as in a trance.

Perhaps the expression "God-breathed" might convey this idea. The line is a fine one. The Spirit is moving, and writers, as Peter says, were indeed "carried along," but we need not infer from this that they were sleep-writing or under some kind of a Spirit-induced hypnosis. The great diversity of literary styles disproves this. Even the handling of Greek is more elegant in Luke than in John, reflecting a superior education. And Luke frankly declares that he carefully researched his materials before presuming to write his account (Luke 1:1-4).

As for the Old Testament, there is every reason to suppose that Moses and other writers drew on oral tradition or previously written documents for some of their material. This does not rule out the direct revelation by the Spirit in matters where no other source of information was available.[5]

QUESTION: *What is the other extreme to be avoided?*

ANSWER: It is a too elastic interpretation of the "dynamic theory." This is sometimes understood to mean that only the thoughts were inspired in the minds of the writers, who were then left "on their own" to express the thoughts as accurately as they knew how. This means that the end product—the Book we hold in our hands—was only indirectly inspired. For the "thoughts" died with the writers, and what we have is a human and fallible attempt to express them. As a result, we are left with the temptation to second-guess what the original thoughts were and to think of ways whereby the writers might have expressed them better. In other words, we are left free to criticize the end product.[6]

QUESTION: *Is there a safer road to take?*

ANSWER: Yes. A safer (and truer) doctrine of inspiration is the belief that while an author used secondary sources and wrote freely in his or her own style, the Holy Spirit so guided the writer's thinking and writing that the accuracy of the teaching God intended was assured—even to the very words. Has not every Spirit-filled preacher at times been aware of receiving words as he or she preaches? Sometimes an unexpected word comes "out of the blue," expressing precisely a crucial note of truth. The preacher is not writing (or speaking) new Scripture but is aware of being free in his or her own personality and at the same time being "carried along" by the Spirit. Admittedly there is a mystery here, but we must try to strike a middle ground between a belief in extreme dictation and a loose dynamic theory, which inevitably leads to biblical fallibility.

We must remember that interpretation requires exegesis, and exegesis is the study of words, not to correct them, but to understand them. And the truly Evangelical approach is to respect the words (in the original languages) as being the right ones.

The blunt truth is that now, 2,000 or more years later, we have no basis for presuming to correct or improve either on the Bible's teaching or the language in which it is couched. It is an affront—and shows incredible conceit—for us to say, "I know this is what Paul says, but I think he misunderstood God's thought, and I think he should have said this instead." We must avoid this approach. If we do not, we may end up becoming revisionists, conforming our revisions to whatever thinking is currently fashionable.

QUESTION: *Is every portion of the Bible equally authoritative over me?*

ANSWER: No. This is where we need to grasp the meaning of 2 Tim. 2:15: "Do your best to present yourself to God as one approved, a workman who does not need to be ashamed and who correctly handles the word of truth." Literally, "correctly handles" means "cutting straight."

The most urgent need for "cutting straight" is between the old and new covenants. But also the interpreter needs to acquire skill in cutting straight between the following distinctions:

Inspiration and revelation. Everything in the Bible is inspired in that it is what God desired as part of the total mosaic, but not everything is in itself revealed truth. This does not mean we are at liberty to treat historical narratives as legend just because some things seem incredible. It merely means some speeches and declarations that are in the Bible do not convey truth, such as the speeches of Job's friends. They made a lot of statements that are not "preachable." God said to Eliphaz and his two friends, "You have not spoken of me what is right" (Job 42:7). So their words do not provide preaching texts just by being in the Bible.

Recording and endorsing. Reporting an action in the Bible, especially the New Testament, should not be interpreted as either a divine endorsement or a prescription for subsequent policy. The Book of Acts, for instance, reports Peter leading the little group in the casting of lots for a successor to Judas, Peter and John observing a 3 P.M. prayer hour, and the Church electing seven deacons. This is reporting, not prescribing. We are not to understand that "casting lots" is the normal way to settle church issues or that 3 P.M. for a prayer meeting is some kind of a secret instruction or that seven deacons is a number "revealed" as God's rule for the Church throughout its history. Principles are revealed here, but not legally prescribed specifics. The *revelation* that underlies these cultural details relates to the basic things. For example, the Church elected deacons to feed widows, the revealed underlying principle being the care of the weak and dependent (James 1:27).

QUESTION: *Are there other distinctions that we need to learn to "cut straight"?*

ANSWER: Yes. Some distinctions are important enough to justify an entire book. The following at least need to be listed:

Law and grace

Promises and their conditions
Commands and their context
Literal and figurative language
The various literary forms
The local and the universal
The passing and the permanent
Cultural variations and basic ethical standards
Optional practical advice and nonoptional mandates

QUESTION: *What is meant by the term "progressive revelation"?*

ANSWER: It is God's gradual self-disclosure. Progressive revelation is clearly declared in Heb. 1:1-2: "In the past God spoke to our forefathers through the prophets at many times and in various ways, but in these last days he has spoken to us by his Son." Judging by the accounts in Genesis, humankind very rapidly degenerated into not only total corruption but also abysmal ignorance of God. God's method of building bridges and reestablishing a relationship with humanity had to be very slow and personalized because of the universal depravity and blindness.

There was gradual movement of revelation from Adam forward—from Enoch to Noah; from Noah to Abraham; then through Moses, Samuel, David, the prophets; and finally, in the "fullness of the time," in the Son (Gal. 4:4, NKJV). God's people slowly gained a better idea of God and also of His intended standards of behavior. There was toleration, for instance, of polygamy in the Old Testament but none in the New. The Bible is the Authoritative Record of this progressive revelation.

QUESTION: *Is the Bible merely a "record" of the revelation?*

ANSWER: No. No one handles this better than James Orr:

We began rightly by distinguishing between revelation and the record of revelation. There is an important truth in that distinction, for it marks the fact that there is an objective revelation in divine acts and words prior to our written record. But we have now found that the line between revelation and its record is becoming very thin, and that, in another true sense, *the record,* in the fulness of its contents, *is itself the revelation. . . .* The record as a whole is the revelation — God's complete word — for us. Its sufficiency is implied in the fact that beyond it we do not need to travel to find God's *whole will* for our salvation.[7]

QUESTION: *Does "progressive revelation" make the Old Testament obsolete?*

ANSWER: Not if we keep in mind the distinction between the Old Testament and the *old covenant,* which was established by Moses at Mount Sinai. The old covenant, not the Old Testament, became obsolete as an organic portion of the Bible. The old covenant was the Mosaic system given to the Israelites in the wilderness as a provision for their spiritual sustenance and preservation. Insofar as the writer to the Hebrews thought of the old covenant as the system of blood sacrifices, Temple worship, and related ritual, he sees it as not only displaced but also destined to oblivion. This idea is given in a nutshell in Heb. 8:13: "By calling this covenant 'new,' he has made the first one obsolete; and what is obsolete and aging will soon disappear."

The passing away of the old covenant included the end of not only the blood sacrifices but also the Judaic priesthood, prescribed feast days, the high Day of Atonement, and dietary restrictions. This exacting cult was designed to discipline the Israelites, to serve as a temporary mode of worship and service, and to serve as a stopgap covering of sin until the Lamb of God should come who would take "away the sin of the world" (John 1:29).

But this does not mean that the Old Testament ceases to be, for us, the Word of God. It was *the Bible* of the Early Church. These are the "holy Scriptures" that were able to make Timothy "wise for salvation," and they are still "useful for teaching, rebuking, correcting and training in righteousness, so that the man of God may be thoroughly equipped for every good work" (2 Tim. 3:15-17). In fact, Paul wrote this long after he knew perfectly well that the Old Testament proscription against pork, for instance, was no longer in force and that circumcision was no longer a requirement for pleasing God.

QUESTION: *How, then, should we approach the Old Testament?*

ANSWER: We should read the Old Testament prayerfully and devotionally but with a sound discernment of those elements not "Christian" and not binding. We can expect God to speak to us through its pages. Old Testament events become the basis of practical lessons for the Christian life. We see an example of this in 1 Cor. 10:1-10 with the Exodus events. Also we are strengthened by dozens of general promises claimable by all of God's people in any age—such as, "Call to me and I will answer you and tell you great and unsearchable things you do not know" (Jer. 33:3). As Haddon Robinson says, "Not all the Bible is written *to* us, but all the Bible is written *for* us."[8]

Our overview of the Bible is neatly summarized by Gerhard Maier:

> Revelation claims to have issued forth from God's Spirit. This revelation, in the context furnished by both Old and New Testaments, is God's address to us. Whoever hears it is hearing first of all not the human authors and witnesses to faith but rather the triune God. Nowhere else can such a trustworthy and adequate message from this God be found. As unique speech from God, it has a unique, incomparable authority. God has bound himself to this word. He has determined that it is the location where he will encounter us. He will vindicate and fulfill this word in every way. The authority of Scripture is, fundamentally, the personal authority of the God who encounters us there.[9]

GOD

What Is the Christian Understanding of God?

QUESTION: *Does the Bible try to prove the existence of God?*

ANSWER: No. It assumes His existence and says simply, "In the beginning God created the heavens and the earth" (Gen. 1:1). The Bible also assumes that a sense of God's reality is written into human nature, as an intuitive knowledge. Paul points out that "what may be known about God is plain to them, because God has made it plain to them. For since the creation of the world God's invisible qualities—his eternal power and divine nature—have been clearly seen, being understood from what has been made, so that men are without excuse" (Rom. 1:19-20).

But in deliberate rebellion men and women may elect to "suppress the truth" (v. 18). The next step is to exchange "the truth of God for a lie" (v. 25). Atheists are those who do "not think it worthwhile to retain the knowledge of God" (v. 28). The consequence is that God gives them "over to a depraved mind" (v. 28).

Modern science is showing that rejection of God is a moral choice, not a scientific or logical necessity. An example is *Darwin's Black Box*, by Michael Behe. This famous biochemist shows conclusively that the amazing structure of the human cell is so intricate that its existence would be impossible without a designer.[1]

QUESTION: *Is God a "person"?*

ANSWER: Some would deny this. Pantheism defines God as the material and spiritual universe. Every person is a part of God, so prayer is just as truly to ourselves as it is to anything outside ourselves. The New Age movement is essentially pantheistic. So is Christian Science. A Christian Science practitioner once asked me, "What is God?" I replied, "Why do you say *what?* Why don't you say *Who?*" Scornfully she exclaimed, "You don't think God is a person, do you?" I assured her that I did.

The Bible presents God as a person—a person who thinks, speaks, acts, feels, and responds, just like men and women who are created in His image. Jesus taught us to pray, "Our Father in heaven, hallowed be your name" (Matt. 6:9). Only a person can be a Father. Only a person can be addressed as "You." Only a person can hear and answer prayer.

QUESTION: *If not the pantheistic view, what is our concept of God?*

ANSWER: We are neither pantheists nor deists, but *theists.* Pantheism has already been explained. *Deism* is the belief that while God is a person and the Creator of all things, He is an absentee God. He has wound up the universe and is letting it run itself while He is busy elsewhere. *Theism,* on the other hand, is the belief that God, as a person and as the Creator, is both *immanent* and *transcendent.* He is immanent because He is omnipresent— present to all of His creation and to all of His creatures. Not only is He "in heaven," but also He is with us, in every worship service, in every problem, in every sorrow, nearer than hands and feet, always ready to hear the cry of His children. He is "the God of all comfort, who comforts us in all our troubles" (2 Cor. 1:3-4). There is no comfort from a God who is busy elsewhere.

But while immanent, God is also transcendent. This means that He is distinct and separate from His creation. He is *above* as well as *with* us. He is not our "buddy" but our majestic Creator God, Ruler over all the earth. Our proper relationship to Him is one of reverence, worship, and obedience.

QUESTION: *What is the most basic truth about the being of God?*

ANSWER: That He is one and yet three. We call Him the Triune God, and we speak of the doctrine of the Holy Trinity. In this Trinity are the Father, the Son, and the Holy Spirit. The Father is God. The Son is God. The Holy Spirit is God. Yet there are not three gods—only one.[2]

QUESTION: *Is anything else essential to this doctrine?*

ANSWER: Yes. It needs also to be stated that these three are co-equal in essential being and coeternal in existence. This means that this is the way God simply *is* and has always been. No one member of this Trinity is subsequent to the others. None has been *created*.

QUESTION: *What is the error of unitarianism concerning this?*

ANSWER: It is that the Son was the first created being. This is argued from the biblical expressions that designate Jesus as the "only begotten," which the unitarians (following Arius, about A.D. 256—336) interpret as meaning that the Son was begotten at a point in time. This was early rejected by the Church as a fatal breach of the Bible teaching. "Only begotten" is better understood as "one and only begotten." The "begetting" is to be understood, not in the same way as the sexual generation of offspring, but as referring to the *eternal and continuous* generation of the Son out of the Father. In ways we cannot fathom, the Son never ceases to be *in* the Father yet never ceases to be distinct from the Father, having a personal center of self-consciousness.

QUESTION: *What Bible passages imply this Trinity?*

ANSWER: One is Matt. 3:16-17, which describes the baptism of Jesus: "As soon as Jesus was baptized, he went up out of the water. At that moment heaven was opened, and he saw the Spirit of God descending like a dove and lighting on him. And a voice from heaven said, 'This is my Son, whom I love; with him I am well pleased.'" Here are three distinct participants: Jesus, the One being baptized; the Spirit, the One coming upon Him in the form of a dove; and God the Father, whose voice is heard identifying Jesus as His Son.

Another passage is from the teaching of Jesus himself, as found in His Upper Room discourse, John 14—16. A careful reading of this discourse will show how Jesus interweaves the functions and Persons of the Trinity so as to present a total unity of action while preserving the distinctiveness of the Persons. After promising the Holy Spirit, He says, "My Father will love him [the believer], and we will come to him and make our home with him" (John 14:23). Here is a Trinity of inward residence in the believer. This "threeness" is seen also in verse 26: "But the Counselor, the Holy Spirit, whom the Father will send in my name, will teach you all things and will remind you of everything I have said to you." Here is oneness of action carried out by three Persons.

QUESTION: *Do we find this teaching in the writings of Paul?*

ANSWER: Yes, in many places. Let us look at two. The Trinity is clearly implied in his wonderful prayer for the Ephesians (Eph. 3:14-21). He directs the prayer to "the Father" (v. 14). He prays for the indwelling strengthening of the Holy Spirit (v. 16). His objective is "that Christ may dwell in your hearts through faith" (v. 17).

Unmistakable is the benediction of 2 Cor. 13:14: "May the grace of the Lord Jesus Christ, and the love of God, and the fellowship of the Holy Spirit be with you all." The love from which redemption originates is ascribed to God the Father; the grace made available is traced to the Son; the personal intimacy of fellowship is through the Holy Spirit. These three act as one—as in fact they are—yet they are distinct.

QUESTION: *Where else is a declaration of the three coequal Persons in the one God?*

ANSWER: In the Great Commission. After the Resurrection Jesus commanded His disciples: "All authority in heaven and on earth has been given to me. Therefore go and make disciples of all nations, baptizing them in the name of the Father and of the Son and of the Holy Spirit" (Matt. 28:18-19).

QUESTION: *Are there analogies that help us understand?*

ANSWER: Yes, but no analogy is perfect. A common metaphor is the family. Assuming two parents and one child, we have three persons in one social unit. To press this analogy too far, however, is to end up with tritheism, the age-old heresy of three gods. I once heard an enthusiastic young preacher declare, "We believe in God; in fact we have three gods!" His very limited theological training was showing! The doctrine of the Trinity is certainly not a belief in three gods. Christianity is as truly monotheistic as Judaism. It is neither polytheistic (belief in many gods) nor tritheistic (belief in three gods). The teaching is that within the one God is a Trinity of Persons.

Yet the Persons are not three separate individuals, as in the human family. The human family can be torn apart by disunity, divorce, or death. That is not possible within the Godhead. Rather the Persons in the Trinity are coinherent in such a way that while distinct they are one and act together.

QUESTION: *How can the doctrine of the Trinity be illustrated?*

ANSWER: Mathematically while $1 + 1 + 1 = 3$, $1 \times 1 \times 1 = 1$. That at least illustrates how something can be both three and one. But more to the point is the following: A cube has three dimensions—width, height, depth. They are distinct. Yet at any point in the cube the dimension of width is also a point on the dimension of height, and points of width and height are also points of depth. In a similar way the three Persons of the Trinity are in and through each other as one God. Yet the analogy falls short because the Godhead is not comprised of three dimensions but three Persons, who know their respective identities yet identify consciously with each other. We must accept the humbling verdict that the reality of the Trinity is beyond human understanding.

QUESTION: *Are some analogies especially to be avoided?*

ANSWER: Yes. Perhaps the most common one is illustrated by a confession made in class by one of my theology teachers, Edward Mott. As a young pastor he felt he had made a great discovery, so he illustrated the Trinity one Sunday morning by saying, "The Trinity is like a single head with three faces. The head turns to show the face of the Father, then turns to show the face of the Son, then turns to show the face of the Holy Spirit." After this a layman said to him, "That is the first time I ever heard the doctrine explained in a way that I could understand." Then Mott exploded to the class, "The only trouble with it was, there wasn't a bit of truth in it!"

His picture reflected a concept of the Trinity that is called modalism. This means that instead of three Persons, there is only one, and this one reveals himself successively as Father, Son, and Holy Spirit. The one Person first revealed himself in the *mode* of Father, then revealed himself in the *mode* of Son, then revealed himself in the *mode* of Spirit. This fails to harmonize with Jesus' words when He said, "Father, into your hands I commit my spirit" (Luke 24:46); He was not speaking to himself, but to One distinct from himself.

QUESTION: *In what ways are the three distinct from each other?*

ANSWER: In two ways. First, they are forever distinct in personal identity. This means that fellowship and communion existed within the Godhead before creation began. Because of this, God's love has always had an object. God didn't need to create humankind for Him to be loving. The Father always loved the Son and the Spirit; the Son and Spirit always loved each other; and the Son and Spirit always loved the Father.

The second way the three are distinct is in their functions, or offices. The Father is the Source of all things; the Son is the Word of the Father by which all things are brought into being; the Spirit is the Agent of change. As the Spirit brooded over the waters in the primeval state (Gen. 1:2), so it is He who holds life together. He is the Immediate Agent in healings and other miracles. But more than this, the Spirit is the Executive Agent in the internal changes that we call awakening, conviction, regeneration, and sanctification. In the words of Gerald Bray, the Holy Spirit is "the one who makes the work of the other two persons real in our lives."[3] Furthermore, He is the Spirit of revelation. He inspired the Holy Scriptures and illuminates our minds to understand them.

These distinctions in function or office constitute what theologians call the *economic* Trinity.

QUESTION: *Isn't this "economic" Trinity the same as modalism?*

ANSWER: No. Modalism stresses the oneness of God in such a way as to cancel His eternal threeness. The economic Trinity is a threefoldness in the *functions* of the three Persons.

QUESTION: *How important is the doctrine of the Trinity?*

ANSWER: It is fundamental to the integrity of Christianity. The plan of salvation requires a Father-God who loves enough to sacrifice His one and only Son, allowing the Second Person of the Trinity to step out of the idyllic harmony of heaven to become human, in order to make an atonement for human sin (Phil. 2:5-11). The plan of salvation also requires a God-the-Son who voluntarily becomes the sacrificial offering. As a man He had real blood to shed, but as God His blood was of infinite value, sufficient to compensate for the sin of the whole world. But further, the plan of salvation also requires a Holy Spirit who, as God invisible and universal, makes the sinner aware of his or her offenses against the holy God; reveals the Son to the sinner; infuses the sinner with prevenient grace; and changes the responding sinner's very character from the inside out.

QUESTION: *Didn't the Incarnation introduce a fracture into the Trinity?*

ANSWER: Not a fracture, but a change. H. Orton Wiley says that the conception in the womb of Mary was "the conjoining of the divine and human natures in a new order of being—a thean-thropic person."[4] He also says, "It was not that which was common to the three persons who assumed our human nature, but that which marks the distinctions in the Trinity. It was not the Godhead which became incarnate, but one of the persons of the Godhead. It was not the Father or the Spirit who became incarnate, but the Son—the Second Person of the Trinity."[5] ("Incarnation" means "enfleshment"—the Son becoming flesh and blood as a true man.)

Jesus will never lay aside His human nature. Before the Incarnation there was no God-Man in the Trinity; now there is. The Incarnation was a radical and real space-time event in human history. Its date divides history into B.C. and A.D. Before that, it was potential in the mind of the Father but not actual. Nor would it ever have become actual if it had not been for the sin that necessitated a Savior from heaven.

Since the Incarnation did not diminish the Son's "Godness" as the eternal Second Person or alter His essential relation to the Father and the Spirit, the Trinity in that sense remains the same. Yet because the Son took into himself human nature, literally becoming a man, a new dimension was introduced into the Godhead. This will always remain and forever affect what it means for God to be God. If this seems to challenge the doctrine of God's immutability, or unchangeableness, it can only be said that the true immutability of God includes an eternal capacity to do whatever is necessary, even within His own being, to accomplish the redemption of a derelict humanity.

QUESTION: *Do we see this change within the Trinity even more clearly in Christ's death?*

ANSWER: Yes. This is shown by three sayings of Jesus on the Cross. One is, "Father, forgive them, for they do not know what they are doing" (Luke 23:34). Here we see that the distinction between the Father and the Son is intact. The Father is not on the Cross but is the One being propitiated, or appeased, for the sins of the world and who alone has the right to grant forgiveness. Jesus died to make it morally possible for this holy God to be generous with His forgiveness.

The second revealing statement was His loud cry, "Father, into your hands I commit my spirit" (Luke 23:46). This was the last breath of the Son's submission to the Father in His redemptive mission (cf. Phil. 2:5-11). But three hours earlier, about noon, He had let out a cry not of confidence but poignant agony: "My God, my God, why have you forsaken me?" (Mark 15:34).

Although Jesus was quoting the opening lines of the messianic Ps. 22, this does not relieve us from seeing in this cry something dreadful transpiring between the Father and the Son. For an eternal Son, who had also become a human, earthly Son, the only normal and natural relationship with the Father that had ever existed had been perfect harmony and exquisite fellowship. But for the first time from all eternity the Son experienced a rupture, a separation, a sense of outpoured wrath, because the Father saw in Jesus all the horrible sins of the world and turned His face. In a sense Jesus, while innocent, was nevertheless taking the *blame* for your sins and mine and suffering the wrath of a holy God as if the sins were His own. In this hour Jesus experienced indescribable agony of spirit, far more excruciating than the mere physical sufferings — as horrible as those were.

So at least in this moment, there was a trauma in the Holy Trinity. The inner wound within the Trinity will be forever. The repeated calling of the Son "the Lamb" in the Book of Revelation is an eternal reminder to the redeemed of what their redemption cost the Father, Son, and Holy Spirit.

QUESTION: *Why were the baptisms recorded in Acts done in the name of Jesus, when Jesus had instructed baptizing in the name of the Father and of the Son and of the Holy Spirit?*

ANSWER: Because the identity of Jesus was the crux of the gospel preaching. The Jews had no question about God, and they also had some knowledge from the Scriptures of the Spirit of God, but it was Jesus whom they had rejected and crucified. Real conversion turned on whether they were willing to identify themselves in public baptism with Jesus as the risen Lord and promised Messiah.

However, a threeness permeates the Book of Acts. In the very first chapter Jesus speaks of the "gift my Father promised" (v. 4), which was the Holy Spirit. Peter, on the Day of Pentecost, speaking of Jesus, said, "Exalted to the right hand of God, he has received from the Father the promised Holy Spirit" (2:33). Here are the Father, the Son, and the Holy Spirit all involved in particular facets of our salvation and all acting as one.

QUESTION: *Can we be saved without believing in the Trinity?*

ANSWER: Getting to heaven does not depend on the total accuracy of our understanding of God. However, we have no ground for hope if we reject the Lord Jesus Christ. Peter said, "Salvation is found in no one else, for there is no other name under heaven given to men by which we must be saved" (Acts 4:12). Paul carried the requirement further: "If you confess with your mouth, 'Jesus is Lord,' and believe in your heart that God raised him from the dead, you will be saved" (Rom.10:9).[6]

SATAN

Where Did the Devil Come from, and What's He Up To?

QUESTION: *Do we really need to know about this to have a proper understanding of Christian theology?*

ANSWER: Yes. Understanding Satan and his kingdom is a core requirement—a Course 101. Without it we cannot really understand what is going on in the moral universe. A crucial key to what the Bible teaches would be missing. D. M. Lloyd-Jones, M.D., says, "The Bible, in a sense, is the record of the conflict between the forces of God and the forces of the devil."[1] To assume that the players are only God and human beings is to try to assemble a puzzle with key pieces still in the box. Much of the story would be totally inexplicable.

QUESTION: *How can the complete picture be stated?*

ANSWER: The complete picture is that of a conflict with three sets of dimensions and four sets of players. Here are the dimensions:

1. **Spiritual/material.** Reality has a spiritual dimension and a material dimension. As human beings we live in both.
2. **Invisible/visible.** The spiritual dimension is invisible but can manifest itself in visible ways. The everyday world perceived by the five senses is the material dimension and also the visible dimension. God has created it and put us into it (Heb. 11:3).
3. **Heavenly/earthly.** The heavenly dimension is the ultimate dimension, embracing the throne of God and the celestial kingdom. This dimension is eternal and foundational. It is the source of all secondary dimensions. The

earthly dimension is the dimension of probation, spatial/temporal/material existence, and temporariness. This earth (at least in present form) is not forever.

QUESTION: *Who are the "four sets of players"?*

ANSWER: They are the following:

1. **The Holy Trinity.** This Trinity we know as Father, Son, and Holy Spirit.
2. **Human beings.** God created them at a historical point, male and female. He created them in His own image—not a physical image—but in the likeness of His personal attributes. Human beings thus possess reason, self-consciousness, a moral nature, freedom, creativity, expression, and love. Having been given freedom to choose, Adam and Eve were first necessarily in a state of probation; that is, they were on trial. Their final character and ultimate destiny were still undecided. It was in their hands. It would be determined by how they used their freedom. Although they failed, probation was extended to their descendants. Thus earthly life for every generation is a trial period.
3. **Angels.** God created these beings. They are basically spirit beings but can manifest themselves visibly. Their probation is past; that is, their final destiny is no longer in doubt.
4. **Satan and demons.** These are also created beings, but they failed in their probation and became totally evil.

QUESTION: *What are the respective parts in this cosmic struggle?*

ANSWER: *Angels* are "ministering spirits sent to serve those who will inherit salvation" (Heb. 1:14). They are commissioned to perform special errands, transmit divine messages, and exercise supernatural power in conflict with the enemy and in the guidance and protection of God's children. Our peril today is "angelolatry"—the worship of angels (one of the tricks of the devil masquerading as an angel of light).

Satan and his legions of demons are anti-God and seek in every possible way to embarrass God, thwart and frustrate His plans, defile and destroy His creation, and above all defeat Him by corrupting the human race, God's crowning handiwork. Satan now knows that the throne is not within his grasp, but he can do much to disrupt and destabilize the moral order.[2]

Human beings are the prize in this awful struggle. Both sides—God and Satan—want their allegiance. Since human beings are free to choose, they determine in the end on whose side they will spend eternity. Nothing less than their eternal destiny is at stake.

The Triune God is the Creator, the rightful Governor, the just Judge, the offended Sovereign, and the merciful Redeemer, exercising all the attributes of these respective roles in a perfect intrapersonal harmony. This Triune God will determine the final outcome of the war, but with mixed results. Some "spoils" will go to Satan because some humans have chosen to go with Satan. Multiplied millions of others will choose to let Christ rescue them from Satan's clutches and will spend eternity rejoicing in heaven (Rev. 7).

QUESTION: *What are some key moments in biblical history when an adversary plays a major role in what is going on?*

ANSWER: First is the temptation in the Garden of Eden, an event contaminating everything that follows in human history. That Satan possessed and used for a mouthpiece this smooth-talking serpent can hardly be doubted in the light of Rev. 12:9: "The great dragon was hurled down—that ancient serpent called the devil, or Satan, who leads the whole world astray."

Second is the remarkable drama found in the Book of Job.[3] Satan accused Job of serving God only because God was prospering and protecting him. God decided to prove Satan wrong by allowing Job to be tested.

Nothing is more basic in the whole of biblical revelation than the proposition that human beings can, by the grace of God, be holy. Adam and Eve failed the test, but Job did not. He proved that holiness can be real—that devotion to God can be given out of pure love for God himself. In other words, Job was not being "good" to get God to bless him. In this demonstration of integrity God was glorified and Satan proven wrong. Moreover, Job stands as a rebuke to every believer in God since who complains that consistent holiness is too much to expect.

QUESTION: *Does the trial of Job throw any light on the suffering of God's people?*

ANSWER: Yes. While this event does not explain all suffering, it suggests an explanation for some of it. The existence of an invisible enemy that is allowed to attack us and test us to the limit may explain some of the mysterious hardships experienced by God's people. Many painful events would be quite inscrutable if God and human beings were the only actors. The highest possible level of demonstrated grace is in the patient endurance and unswerving loyalty of buffeted saints when they cannot make sense out of what is happening to them. The "health, wealth, and prosperity" advocates talk about "grace," but they know little of its depths.

QUESTION: *Are there other revealing passages in the Old Testament?*

ANSWER: Yes, two more can be cited. First is the insight given in Dan. 10:12-13. The angel explained his delay in reaching Daniel by saying, "The prince of the Persian kingdom resisted me twenty-one days. Then Michael, one of the chief princes, came to help me." Here we have spiritual conflict in the cosmic realm between two mighty forces, God's messengers and Satan's opposition. How such a battle could be waged is a mystery to us, but obviously the Bible intends that we take this event seriously and at face value.

Second is the confrontation in Zech. 3:1-2. "Then he showed me Joshua the high priest standing before the angel of the LORD, and Satan standing at his right side to accuse him." Here we see Satan taking the role of prosecuting attorney (cf.

Rev. 12:10). What was God's response? "The LORD said to Satan, 'The LORD rebuke you, Satan! The LORD, who has chosen Jerusalem, rebuke you!'" God is the only rightful prosecuting attorney. God claims all such prerogatives for himself, and He will not surrender a single inch to an imposter. All Satan can do is accuse, but God through His Son pardons. Jesus has already paid the penalty (and the benefits reach all the way back to Adam as well as all the way down to us). The benefits can be forfeited only by letting Satan rule us instead of God.

QUESTION: *Are there significant turning points also in the New Testament?*

ANSWER: Yes. The most important is the temptation of Jesus in the wilderness (Matt. 4:1-11; cf. Luke 4:1-13). Clearly this was not a series of subjective suggestions arising from within Jesus, but an exchange with another person. The Gospel writers refer to this person as "the devil" (*diabolos*, one who speaks against), but Jesus speaks directly to him by name: "Away from me, Satan!" (Matt. 4:10).

Also there is the dialogue between Jesus and the Pharisees over the exorcising of demons (Matt. 12:22-32). The Pharisees believed in the reality of demons and demon possession; that was not at issue. But to avoid the plain implications of Christ's power over demons, they rashly and blasphemously declared, "This fellow does not cast out demons except by Beelzebub, the ruler of the demons" (v. 24, NKJV). This prompted Jesus not only to expose the fallacy of their reasoning but also to warn against the unforgivable sin—the blasphemy against the Holy Spirit, that is, ascribing to the devil the work of God. The point, however, is that both parties believed that Satan was a real person and a real power.

Less obvious but nevertheless significant is the revelation given by Jesus in His parable of the weeds (Matt. 13:24-30). After the farmer had sowed seed and while "everyone was sleeping, his enemy came and sowed weeds among the wheat" (v. 25). When the weeds appeared while the wheat was growing, the farmer simply said, "An enemy did this" (v. 28). Jesus is implying that as God looks out across the world and sees the weeds of sin—the carnage and depravity—He says, "An enemy did this." The debauchery and cruelty of the world cannot be blamed on God.

Finally, the last chapters of the Bible show the age-old conflict coming to its eternal resolution. This includes the binding of Satan for a thousand years and his final, irrevocable destruction in the "lake of burning sulfur" (Rev. 20:2, 10). In verse 2 we read, "He seized the dragon, that ancient serpent, who is the devil, or Satan, and bound him for a thousand years." In verse 10 we read, "And the devil, who deceived them, was thrown into the lake of burning sulfur." Here again the names dragon, serpent, devil, and Satan are assigned to one person, designated by the personal pronoun "him."

QUESTION: *How is Satan's character described in the Scriptures?*

ANSWER: Jesus explains to His listeners in John 8:44, "He [the devil] was a murderer from the beginning, not holding to the truth, for there is no truth in him. When he lies, he speaks his native language, for he is a liar and the father of lies." In Rev. 12 the "dragon" cast out of heaven with his "angels" is identified as "that ancient serpent called the devil, or Satan, who leads the whole earth astray" (vv. 7-9). He is also called "the accuser of our brothers, who accuses them before our God day and night" (v. 10).

Revelation references the deceiving nature of Satan's activity at least five times. He is said to lead "the whole world astray" (12:9). He "deceived the inhabitants of the earth" by his miraculous signs (13:14). In chapter 20 he is locked up during the millennium "to keep him from deceiving the nations anymore"; when released at the end of the thousand years, he will again seek to "deceive the nations" (vv. 3, 7). Again, "the devil, who deceived them, was thrown into the lake of burning sulfur" (v. 10). It was by deception that he captured Eve, and deception always has been and still is his primary strategy.

As a deceiver Satan is a master at
  making wrong appear right and right appear wrong;
  promising freedom through sinning;
  captivating the unwary by a veneer of righteousness;
  painting the pleasures of sin in glowing colors and disguising consequences;
  persuading nations that *might* makes *right*;
  convincing people that moral expediency is a legitimate strategy;
  and devising many other such deceits by which he keeps the multitudes under his thumb.

In sum, recognition is interwoven throughout all the Scriptures of an enemy, with whom God and the forces of righteousness—including God's people—are waging an uncompromising war. Remove this strain of truth from the Bible, and the Bible loses its coherence.

QUESTION: *Could God have created humankind to provide a counterpoint to Satan?*

ANSWER: Nowhere does the Bible say this. Yet Oswald Chambers conjectured, "God created man to counteract the devil." If so, God lost the first round in the fight. But it will be Christ-redeemed men and women, sanctified, Spirit-empowered, diligent, fervent, and obedient, whom God will use to destroy the kingdom of darkness and hasten the eternal collapse of Satan's power. Every Christian who is an overcomer significantly weakens Satan's grip on the world. Every battle won against temptation blunts Satan's arrows and counteracts to some degree the calamitous consequences of Adam's sin. The first Adam surrendered the world to the devil; the second Adam came to "destroy the works of the devil" (1 John 3:8, NKJV).

QUESTION: *Does the reality of Satan shed light on the origin of evil?*

ANSWER: Yes. Biblically we know that moral evil did not begin with Adam and Eve, for a moral agent who already was evil—

the serpent—tempted them. How did the serpent become the bearer of evil? If the Bible did not reveal the prior presence of Satan, our query would be roadblocked. Our speculation would probably yield some form of metaphysical dualism—the belief that spirit and matter, together with light and darkness and good and evil, are coeternal. But biblical religion is not dualistic. "In the beginning God created the heavens and the earth" (Gen. 1:1; cf. Col. 1:16). Only two realities exist—God and His creation. And "creation"—that is, the universe including personal beings—is dependent every instant on God's patient tolerance.

QUESTION: *To what can we trace the evil in Satan?*

ANSWER: To him alone. Moral evil originates in the misuse of free will. Only a free will can commit sin and create moral evil. In no sense can God ever be blamed for sin. "The origin of evil is in the misuse of freedom," writes Norman Geisler.[4]

QUESTION: *Are there clues in the Bible concerning Satan's fall?*

ANSWER: Yes. Jesus said, "I saw Satan fall like lightning from heaven" (Luke 10:18). As we have already seen, the same event is noted in Rev. 12: "And there was war in heaven. Michael and his angels fought against the dragon, and the dragon and his angels fought back. But he was not strong enough, and they lost their place in heaven. The great dragon was hurled down" (vv. 7-9). "The accuser . . . has been hurled down" (v. 10). "He had been hurled to the earth" (v. 13). Four times the graphic word "hurled" is used, suggesting violent and decisive expulsion. Peter caps these words by writing that "God did not spare angels when they sinned, but sent them to hell, putting them into gloomy dungeons to be held for judgment" (2 Pet. 2:4; cf. Jude 6).

QUESTION: *What are some clear implications of these passages?*

ANSWER: Four implications stand out:
First, Satan and his angels are *created beings* and were thus

created holy but apparently on probation. They had free wills and were capable of rebelling against God.

Second, their rightful place was *heaven*, where clearly Satan was a leader among other angelic leaders.

Third, the eruption of war in heaven could only imply *mutiny* on the part of some of these free moral agents, with Satan as the leader. Other hints in the Bible suggest the rise of pride in Satan's heart, with the dream of dethroning God and reigning in His place. John Milton's *Paradise Lost* is a poetically moving, exciting account of how this might have happened.[5]

Fourth, the conquest and expulsion of Satan and his angels suggests that Satan is already a *defeated foe* and that his rebellion against God is futile. Jesus did not die primarily to conquer the devil—God's power settled that—but to rescue humanity from its own sin and from Satan's bondage. John says Jesus came to "destroy the devil's work" (1 John 3:8).

QUESTION: *Are Satan and his demons redeemable?*

ANSWER: No. As an archangel in heaven, Satan was without excuse. When he rebelled, he not only chose evil but became evil—absolute evil, just as truly as God is absolute good. In thus becoming the very essence of evil, he lost the knowledge of the good. C. S. Lewis suggests that he has no concept of love and is therefore suspicious of God's kind treatment of human beings, wondering what He "is up to." Screwtape says to his nephew Wormwood, "All His talk about Love must be a disguise for something else—He must have some *real* motive for creating them and taking so much trouble about them." Then he bewails "our utter failure to find out that real motive. What does He stand to make out of them? That is the insoluble question."[6] It was this total lack of understanding that led Satan to double-cross himself by seeking the crucifixion of Jesus. Satan entered into Judas to prompt him to betray the Lord. If Satan had really realized that this would result in the deliverance of his captives, he would have done all that was possible to prevent the Crucifixion.

QUESTION: *Why was Satan allowed to tempt Adam and Eve?*

ANSWER: Satan's access to the garden was made necessary because the human pair was being put under trial. The spontaneous holiness of heart with which they were created had to be tested. They needed an opportunity to turn primitive holiness into holiness of character by a confirming choice in the face of powerful temptation. Satan was tempting them to think that disobedience would be a harmless way to enlarge their freedom and improve their status. Unfortunately they gave in to the temptation.

QUESTION: *What effect did Adam's fall have on Satan's earthly power?*

ANSWER: Instead of establishing his character in holiness and validating his role as God's appointed ruler over the earth, Adam surrendered both himself and his official role into Satan's hands. If Adam had refused to sin, Satan's power would in all likelihood have been broken on the spot. Instead, in some mysterious way, Adam's fall delivered this planet and its inhabitants into Satan's control. Because Adam despised the suzerainty intended for him, Satan claimed it as his by default.

This is the only way we can explain why Paul referred to Satan as "the god of this world" (2 Cor. 4:4, NASB) and "the prince of the power of the air" (Eph. 2:2, NKJV). "The whole world," writes John, "is under the control of the evil one" (1 John 5:19). Satan's offer to turn over to Jesus all the kingdoms of the world in exchange for worshiping him was not an idle promise. And with insidious acceleration the culture of the last days will be dominated by Satan's hordes. The captured will include professing Christians: "The Spirit clearly says that in later times some will abandon the faith and follow deceiving spirits and things taught by demons" (1 Tim. 4:1).

QUESTION: *Is Satan's freedom to harass unlimited?*

ANSWER: No. While Satan is permitted to oppress humanity—thanks to human wills in cooperation with him—he is nevertheless divinely restrained. He was with Job. He was also with Peter.

Jesus said to Peter, "Simon, Simon, Satan has asked to sift you as wheat. But I have prayed for you, Simon, that your faith may not fail" (Luke 22:31-32).

The crucial point is that Satan's attack on Peter was both with Christ's permission and with Christ's restraint. Without doubt, so was his attack on Eve. And today also, Satan's destructive power is great, but he wears a leash with the other end held by God. In His administration God chooses to use a wicked devil to accomplish, not the devil's ends, but His own. So we, like Peter and like Job, are being sifted frequently by the devil, with Christ's permission. When this happens, we also can be sure, not of Christ's desertion, but of His intercession for us, *by name.*

QUESTION: *How crucial is humanity's part in this cosmic conflict?*

ANSWER: Humanity's part is major. Just as Adam and Eve's disobedience embarrassed God and delivered this planet into Satan's domination, so will Adam and Eve's redeemed descendants be used by God to recover this planet and bring about Satan's eternal downfall. Just as an archangel became Satan by the misuse of free will, so the proper use of free will by human beings, redeemed and sanctified by the blood of Jesus, will be God's primary weapon in breaking the hold of Satan. As we exercise our freedom to pray, believe, and obey, we bring into the plan "divine power to demolish strongholds" (2 Cor. 10:4-6). It is still true:

> *Satan trembles when he sees*
> *The weakest saint upon his knees.*

Every human will devoted fully to God and His will is a loosening of the fabric of evil. Through this we can aid in bringing about Satan's eternal and final downfall. There is even a hint that we may not only personally be prepared for "the day of God" but also "speed its coming" (2 Pet. 3:12). This makes us coworkers with God at a much deeper level than we had realized. This incredible responsibility—and privilege—should fill us with awe and prompt renewed resolution to be valiant warriors for God.

GOD'S SOVEREIGNTY
Can God's Sovereignty Be Thwarted?

QUESTION: *How can sovereignty be defined?*

ANSWER: It is God's *right* to rule over the universe and everything in it. That includes you and me. This right is absolute (without limitations).

QUESTION: *What is the basis of God's sovereignty?*

ANSWER: God's right to rule rests on three facts:

First, He alone is God; that is, there are no legitimate rival authorities.

Second, He is the Creator of all things. One who creates owns the creation and the right to control it. "Everything under heaven belongs to me," said God to Job (Job 41:11).

Third, God's power, wisdom, justice, and benevolence are fully equal to the demands of ruling and thus qualify Him for the claim of absolute authority. His power is more than adequate to back up His claim. He can do anything His sovereign will chooses to do. "Is anything too hard for the LORD?" (Gen. 18:14; see also Luke 1:37).

QUESTION: *Is God's sovereignty limited in any way?*

ANSWER: Yes. While His *right* and His *power* to rule are unlimited, three things control His *use* of that right:

First, His own holiness limits His sovereignty. This is our assurance that God's sovereignty will be exercised righteously. "Will not the Judge of all the earth do right?" queries Abraham in his intercession for Sodom (Gen. 18:25).

Second, the exercise of divine sovereignty is limited by divine love. When the scripture declares "God is love" (1 John 4:16), we are to understand that God never asserts His sovereignty in any way but lovingly. Even behind His judgments is His love. He rules to save and bless. This is our assurance against a tyrannical kind of sovereignty, such as is commonly found among earthly sovereigns. "He cannot disown himself" (2 Tim. 2:13); that is, He cannot contradict His loving and holy nature.

Third—and this is one of Christian theology's fundamental pillars—He has limited the exercise of His sovereignty by the creation of free wills.

QUESTION: *Then can divine sovereignty be thwarted?*

ANSWER: No, His sovereignty cannot be thwarted, but His *will* can be. If this doesn't seem to make sense, just wait. Things will become clearer as we move along.

The moment God created men and women with power to think and act for themselves, He created the possibility of being rejected. God set up a moral relationship with these free beings in which He might not always have His way. It was not God's will that Adam and Eve eat of the forbidden fruit. But God gave them a nature that had the power to do it, in spite of God's will. This is what it means to be a free moral agent.

Not only so, but also God's *will* is for all people to be saved (1 Tim. 2:3-4; 2 Pet. 3:9; John 3:16). But not all will be. Every lost soul sent to hell at the Judgment will be a sad defeat of what God really wanted (Matt. 25:46; Rom. 2:4-5; see also Matt. 23:37-38). Moreover, Jesus taught us to pray, "Your kingdom come, your will be done on earth as it is in heaven" (Matt. 6:10). If God's perfect will is already being done on earth, why this prayer?

QUESTION: *Can human wills interfere with God's specific will for a specific situation?*

ANSWER: Yes. A perfect example is the case of Ahab setting Ben-Hadad free and the resulting judgment voiced by the prophet: "You have set free a man I had determined should die" (1 Kings

20:42). God's will was defeated by Ahab's ill-advised leniency. Then there was King Josiah. He was only 39 years of age when the Egyptian army killed him, because he stubbornly refused to "listen to what Neco had said at God's command" (2 Chron. 35:22). It was not God's will that Josiah die so prematurely, at the height of his great religious reforms.

QUESTION: *Then is this not a thwarting of God's sovereignty?*

ANSWER: No, because God *in His sovereignty* established this precarious situation of freedom and risk. God elected to create a free being rather than a robot because He wanted a *person* with whom He could have fellowship. Real heart-to-heart fellowship with a robot is impossible. Puppets dancing on a divine string would not glorify God, but the loving devotion of free children does. Equally, their free disobedience grieves and disappoints God.[1]

QUESTION: *Why doesn't God force people to do right?*

ANSWER: Exercising His sovereignty by coercion (or by irresistibly overpowering the human will) would cancel all moral value in their "devotion." Love cannot be coerced. Neither can true obedience be coerced. Forced obedience is external only; it's not from the heart and not voluntary and therefore not true obedience. Every parent knows that a child may be conforming outwardly but seething inwardly. But "obedience" that is either forced or yielded hypocritically to gain advantage is without virtue or value. What parent is satisfied with it? And if parents are not satisfied with this kind of "obedience," why should we expect God to be?

Because God himself has given human beings real moral freedom, they are capable of resisting His claims. Their resistance is not a thwarting of sovereignty, for their ability to resist has been given to them *by that sovereignty.* Allowing humans to rebel is not a defeat of God's sovereignty but an *exercise of it.* As sovereign, God has the *right* to establish a plan that includes real freedom.

QUESTION: *Is this an answer to the frequent complaint, "Why doesn't God do something?"*

ANSWER: Yes. It helps us to keep God's methods in perspective. He *is* doing something—always—but not always what our little minds think He ought to be doing.

   If God will not compel humans to serve Him, neither will He prevent wicked persons from being wicked. He will at times restrain or block them for the sake of His children and for the sake of His world plans, but He will not arbitrarily change their hearts. Therefore it is a complete mistake to suppose that for God to be truly sovereign, His will must always be done.[2]

QUESTION: *What is the danger of thinking that to preserve God's sovereignty, His exact will must always be done?*

ANSWER: Such thinking leads to the notion that lost souls are lost, not ultimately because of their own choice, but because God *sovereignly* predestined them to be lost. Some would object to this blunt way of putting it, preferring to say people are finally lost because God sovereignly chose not to elect them to salvation. He merely left them to the just outcome of their own wickedness. But when you boil it down, the meaning is the same.

QUESTION: *But doesn't our disobedience somehow cripple God's sovereignty?*

ANSWER: No. Disobedience neither cancels nor reduces divine sovereignty. All of the rights and powers of God's sovereignty remain intact. He only asks that we come under that sovereignty willingly. Refusal to come under it is what sin is. God will exercise His sovereignty in calling, commanding, and bringing the influence of the Holy Spirit upon us but will always stop short of compelling us. If we continue to resist, He will exercise His sovereignty by bringing us under the rod of judgment; and if that doesn't work, He will ultimately banish us forever from His presence. Thus His sovereignty is neither surrendered nor compromised. But we will cover more of this later.

QUESTION: *If humans can and do resist God, why do we keep saying that "God is in control"? Isn't that "whistling in the dark"?*

ANSWER: No, because God always knows what to do next. He doesn't surrender the reins because He has an unruly horse. He may replace the horse, but He stays in charge. An example is the rebellion of the children of Israel at Kadesh Barnea when God wanted them to invade the Promised Land immediately. "But you were unwilling to go up; you rebelled against the command of the LORD your God," declared Moses (Deut. 1:26). God allowed their rebellion but did not surrender control. Rather, He adjusted His program and sentenced that generation to die in the wilderness. Their 40 years of wandering was not God's primary will, but it demonstrated that in spite of their disobedience He remained in charge.

QUESTION: *Does the parable of the marred vessel in Jer. 18:1-10 help us here?*

ANSWER: Yes. The lesson in this parable is plain. It illustrates God's change of plans concerning a person or nation in response to that person's or nation's stubbornness. The original design of the potter could not be carried out because the clay was marred. There was something unyielding in it. So the potter made a new vessel and thus remained in charge.

But we must not miss the implication here. A new vessel was possible only on the supposition that the potter managed to rid the clay of the resistance. Since literal clay has no say in the matter, it is up to the potter to extract the offending element. But when you and I are the clay, we have a power God has not given to natural clay. We have the power to say no to the potter and refuse to surrender our stubbornness.

What happens then? If we return to the Jeremiah passage, we will make a surprising discovery. God's power to do with people what a potter does with his clay—make a different but perhaps equally beautiful vessel—is contingent on their cooperation, freely given. Look at verses 5-17. Notice how God puts the final issue squarely in the hands of His people: "'So turn from your evil ways, each one of you, and reform your ways and your actions.' But they will reply, 'It's no use. We will continue with our own plans; each of us will follow the stubbornness of his evil heart'" (vv. 11-12). Result? "I will scatter them before their enemies; I will show them my back and not my face in the day of their disaster" (v. 17). No beautiful alternative vessel is here! As C. S. Lewis noted, "There are only two kinds of people in the end: those who say to God, 'Thy will be done,' and those to whom God says, in the end, '*Thy* will be done.'"[3] But even when God reluctantly and sorrowfully concedes to the final verdict of human choice, He remains in charge. He has the last word.

G. Campbell Morgan observes, "There is no escape from the throne of God. The government of God will destroy or make; the government of God will be to me a blasting or a blessing according to my attitude toward that throne. . . . By submission to the throne; by bending before it and kissing the scepter, and yielding our life to it, we put ourselves in right relationship to it, and that government is then beneficent and healing."[4]

QUESTION: *If sovereignty respects the freedom of the will, how can God achieve His final goals?*

ANSWER: It is clear by now that God has two kinds of will—a *desire* will, which we have been talking about, and a *decree* will, which we come to now.

The "desire" will longs for the willing obedience of every human being. This will is compassionate, wooing, yearning, giving—this is what John 3:16 is all about. But the "decree" will is God's determination to bring certain things to pass. The resistance of neither humans nor devils can stop the "decree" will—their resistance can only deprive them of sharing in the blessings.

As we have already explained, God refrains from violating the sacred territory of free choice when final allegiance or refusal of allegiance to Him is at stake. But at all other points He can and does control events. He can influence the minds and wills of sinners and cause them to do things and make decisions that serve God's purposes, apart from the question of their personal salvation. An example is the heathen king Nebuchadnezzar, whom God twice calls "my servant," because he unwittingly carried out God's plans (Jer. 25:9; 27:6).

QUESTION: *What are the decrees God in His divine sovereignty brings to pass independent of any rival or opposing wills?*

ANSWER: The fundamental decree encompasses God's decision to institute a plan of redemption for sinful humanity and the further decision that this plan will have an end in history. Human history will culminate at some future date in a final Judgment, with humans being absorbed into either heaven or hell. Thus history is *teleological*, that is, moving toward a predetermined end.

The plan of redemption provides that all human beings may choose the final destiny of heaven if they will. This is a basic, unchangeable principle. But the unfolding of the plan in history is complex. The study of biblical prophecy is fascinating because we would like to know the details of God's timing. But Jesus explained to His disciples that the "times or dates the Father has set by his own authority" (Acts 1:7).

For the accomplishment of His grand plan God has decreed *means*, *roles*, and *terms*.

QUESTION: *What are the "means" God has decreed for the accomplishment of His redemption?*

ANSWER: The *means* that God has decreed to make eternal salvation possible center on the incarnation of His one and only Son. The Incarnation made it possible for the God-Man, His Son, to die a substitutionary death on the Cross for all people and to release the Cross's power for their redemption by rising from the grave. All other preparatory divine acts converge on this dual event.

The *means* also include the Bible, as God's Word. The Bible can be called a means because it connects humanity with God's will and power. God *works* through the Word for the accomplishment of His ends.

The *means* also include Pentecost, with the outpouring of the Holy Spirit upon Christ's followers, both for purity and for power. The means thus include the Church as Christ's Body on earth and as Christ's agency for the spreading of the gospel to the ends of the earth.

The *means* include prayer, as a study of Acts and the Epistles will confirm. Having urged upon the Ephesians "the full armor of God" (Eph. 6:10-17), Paul climaxes his appeal with this plea: "And pray in the Spirit on all occasions with all kinds of prayer and requests. . . . Pray also for me, that whenever I open my mouth, words will be given me so that I will fearlessly make known the mystery of the gospel" (vv. 18-19).

Preaching is a fundamental *means* in which God invests great power. "God was pleased through the foolishness of what was preached to save those who believe," declares Paul (1 Cor. 1:21). His last admonition to Timothy was, "Preach the Word" (2 Tim. 4:2).

QUESTION: *What is meant by "roles"?*

ANSWER: God has not only decreed the means by which He will implement redemption but also ordained individuals to particular kinds of service and places of labor. This means that God decides who does what in the unfolding of His master plan.

God called Abraham out of Ur of the Chaldeans to become the father of a special people through whom the Scriptures would be given and out of whom the Christ would come.

God elected Moses to be the deliverer and lawgiver. He elected Joshua to lead the people into Canaan. He elected Samuel, calling him even as a small boy. He elected Isaiah, Jeremiah, and all the prophets to be His spokesmen and penmen. He elected John the Baptist to become the forerunner of Jesus. He elected the Virgin Mary to bear the Messiah. He elected Saul to become Paul, the last apostle.

QUESTION: *Could these persons have rejected their roles?*

ANSWER: Yes. Judas rejected his role as an apostle. Demas rejected his role as a called evangelist (see 2 Tim. 4:10). Jesus urged that we pray for the Lord of the harvest to send out workers. Are there no called workers who have rebelled and none who have gone AWOL? The statement above that God's decrees include plans He will not permit to be frustrated needs to be qualified. Are we not to believe that the last 2,000 years of Christian and world history would have been different if every called worker had labored faithfully in the field? Fortunately for us those named in the above paragraph obeyed.

Their "election" was to specific roles, not to final salvation. The salvation of all these people was as dependent on their own voluntary surrender, obedience, and faith as was the salvation of anyone else.

In reaching the world for Christ today, God's sovereign will still determines who will be preachers, pastors, and teachers. The Church is supposed to recognize, endorse, and send, but it is God that calls.

It is equally true with the laity. God's sovereign will determines where and how He wants *anyone* to serve. Therefore our job is to find out what God wants and get on with it.

QUESTION: *Does this mean that God's plan for us is so inflexible that if we miss it, our lives will be wasted?*

ANSWER: No. It simply means that God has a plan for our lives, and it is our duty to seek it. Many Christians have missed the way at some point but have still gone on to find their niche and be greatly used of God. If we remember the parable of the clay and the potter, we will find comfort in knowing that if we cease our stubbornness and become pliable, God can put us back on the track and still mold us into a useful vessel.

QUESTION: *What do we mean by the "terms" God has decreed?*

ANSWER: We mean the conditions God lays out for us to conform to if we are to be eternally saved. All of us are invited, but the acceptance must be on God's terms, not our own. The parable of the wedding garment illustrates this (Matt. 22:1-14). The story concerns the king who planned a great wedding banquet for his son. He first invited the elite, but "they refused to come." However, the king managed to get a full house by sending his servants to gather off the streets anyone they could hustle into the palace.

Apparently each one gathered was supplied with and expected to wear a special wedding garment. This was the condition or the "term" on which each one could stay. The term was not age, wealth, health, intelligence, position, culture, education, appearance, good works, good looks, a good reputation, or even good intentions. It was absolutely none of the values humans would tend to think might entitle a person to stay. But the king set the terms, not the ones gathered, and the wedding garment was mandatory. As a result, the one guest who failed to wear the required garment was peremptorily cast out. Jesus' own application of the parable is, "For many are invited, but few are chosen" (v. 14).

Multitudes try to crowd in for the "goodies" of religion but are not willing to humble themselves in repentance and faith; that is, they are not willing to come to the wedding on the King's terms. They think they can choose their own. But God's terms are inflexible. No one gets to heaven by going around them. They are repentance toward God, faith in Christ, and obedience to Christ and His Spirit (Acts 20:21; 2 Thess. 2:13; Heb. 5:9; 1 Pet. 1:2). Any "faith" that attempts to bypass repentance and obedience is spurious and will leave its possessor as speechless as the man at the wedding. The "terms" therefore belong to the category of God's decrees.

QUESTIONS: *But doesn't the Bible speak of our being "predestinated"?*

ANSWER: Yes, in several places. But this is not an arbitrary predetermination of our personal eternal destiny. It is the destiny God designed for humankind from the beginning—thus it is a "pre-destiny." Adam and Eve's destiny was to populate and subdue and manage this earth as God's stewards, in perfect holiness and fellowship with God and each other. But they "blew it." Their pre-destiny was not fulfilled.

God's backup plan for humankind came through the Cross and provided for the complete recovery of all who would believe. "For God so loved the world that he gave his one and only Son, that whoever believes in him shall not perish but have eternal life" (John 3:16). This is God's declaration concerning every human being—thus it is every person's true destiny. It is what God *predestines* for each of us. But unbelief will forfeit this destiny as surely as Adam and Eve spoiled theirs.

QUESTION: *How does the Bible illustrate the line between God's election by "decree" and His election by grace?*

ANSWER: A helpful example is the Passover, which God provided for the children of Israel in Egypt. They were God's chosen people, elected by decree to be God's instrument in advancing His plan for humankind. They were assigned to cut a special channel in the broad stream of humanity. But this election did not unconditionally guarantee the salvation of each individual. In decreeing the 10th judgment on Pharaoh and his people, God provided an escape for the children of Israel by instructing them to sacrifice lambs and to sprinkle the blood on the lintel and posts of their doors. The decree was, "When I see the blood, I will pass over you" (Exod. 12:13). God was not saying, "When I see an Israelite . . ."; He was saying, "When I see individual Israelites (as heads of households) in *obedience* . . ."

The obedience was not compelled. The guaranteed security was not through some kind of "irresistible grace"—or *infusion* of an obedient heart. The ability to obey or not to obey was assumed. The lamb did not create moral ability. The lamb was a symbol of free obedience, just exactly as was the tree in the Garden of Eden. Each father made up his own mind. God's decree for the nation was a general decree that *was made particular* by those who voluntarily chose to believe and obey.

Believing cannot be severed from obeying. To believe that the death angel was coming and yet do nothing would render the faith useless. To act, that is, to put the blood on the door as instructed, would be not only obeying but also demonstrating belief. A person will not act if he or she does not believe, and a person does not believe effectually if he or she does not act.

God was in charge. He had judged the Egyptians. He told the Israelites how to escape the death angel. But the escape of their families individually did not depend on the sovereignty, will, decree, or power of God but on the personal exercise of absolutely free choice. If there was a division, it was not on the basis of some divine "election" but purely on the basis of human decision.

QUESTION: *How can these truths be "wrapped up"?*

ANSWER: Let us summarize:

- God refuses to use His sovereign power to cut off the power of choice.
- A person's rebellion cannot thwart God's ultimate plan for the world, but it can eliminate that person's participation in it.
- It is not God's will (loving wish) that any free agent rebel against Him, but it is His sovereign will (decree) that those who do rebel against Him shall forfeit the benefits of His redemption.[5]
- God's methods include the initiative of prevenient grace, the conviction of the Holy Spirit, the preaching of the Word, and human and divine persuasion (2 Cor. 5:11); but His grace is not "irresistible."
- God never surrenders His sovereignty. He does not abdicate His throne. He does not allow free agents to reject Him and get away with it. He will hold all free agents He has ever created (humans or angels) accountable for the way they use or misuse free will. "We must all appear before the judgment seat of Christ," Paul declares (2 Cor. 5:10; cf. Heb. 9:27).

I watched a skilled harpist one evening as he drew soul-stirring music from his $8,000 instrument. But the music was made possible not only by the musician's skill but also by the true pitch and responsiveness of every string. Afterward I spoke to the audience.

"Suppose," I said, "these strings were people and had wills of their own. Suppose, when the harpist took out his tuning key and began to adjust them to perfect harmony, one of them should angrily resist and say, 'Hands off! I have my rights. I will not let you change me!' The harpist might reason, cajole, plead, argue. But if the string was adamant, the harpist would finally say, 'Very well, then. Your only value to me is as a string among other strings fastened to this harp and tuned to make music instead of discord. If you refuse to fulfill your destiny, I have no choice but to remove you and toss you away. I have no other use for you. I will replace you with a string that will submit to my control.'"

This is the ultimate word of God to every impenitent, self-willed, unbelieving human soul. What a tragedy! The soul has had its way, but God in His sovereignty has made the final verdict. Neither free will nor divine sovereignty has been violated. Both have been preserved intact but at a terrible cost to the rebellious harp string, which will lie forever on the trash heap of eternity!

DIVINE PROVIDENCE
Does God Cause Everything That Happens to Me?

QUESTION: *What branch of doctrine are we talking about?*

ANSWER: We are looking at the subject of divine providence, one of the most fascinating subjects in all theology. Simply put, it is the doctrine that God is not only the universe's Creator but also its Manager. Macromanagement is Christ "sustaining all things by his powerful word" (Heb. 1:3). Micromanagement is the Father taking note of the falling sparrow (Matt. 10:29).

God created not only the universe but humankind, too, as His showcase masterpiece. So God is also the manager of humankind —even to the numbering of head hairs (Matt. 10:30). It is God's mode of management at the personal, everyday level that sometimes puts a strain on both our understanding and our faith.

QUESTION: *When is God not the cause of what happens to us?*

ANSWER: God permits sin, but He is not its author. The Bible makes this clear: "When tempted, no one should say, 'God is tempting me.' For God cannot be tempted by evil, nor does he tempt anyone" (James 1:13). Since God is never the prompter of sin, He is not responsible for the tragic effects of sin. He may modify them; He may use them; but He did not cause them.

God permits Satan to work. He allowed Satan to deceive Eve, but He did not put Satan up to it. God allowed Joseph's brothers to sell him into slavery, but He did not put the idea into their minds. Their own meanness was sufficient for that. But God permitted it for a long-range purpose, as Joseph explained to his frightened brothers: "But as for you, you meant evil

against me; but God meant it for good, in order to bring it about
as it is this day, to save many people alive" (Gen. 50:20, NKJV).

Because they acted freely and with evil motives, they were
justly under divine condemnation. But God absorbed their evil
deed into His own plan, without making himself responsible for
their wickedness. God was not dependent on their wrongdoing
to accomplish His purpose. He could have gotten Joseph to the
throne of Egypt some other way.

QUESTION: *Does what happened to Job illustrate what God
causes and what He does not?*

ANSWER: Yes. God didn't violently destroy Job's wealth and his
10 children all in one day. Satan did. Neither did God send the
boils that turned life into a living hell. Satan did that too. But
God did keep Satan on a leash: "Everything he has is in your
hands, but on the man himself do not lay a finger" (Job 1:12).
Then when Satan complained about being unfairly restrained,
God let the leash out a little: "The LORD said to Satan, 'Very
well, then, he is in your hands; but you must spare his life" (2:6).
The evil came from Satan—as had the accusation that Job's religion was merely a front.

But because God authorized the test and permitted Satan to
do his cruel work, He could say, "You incited me against him to
ruin him without any reason" (2:3). As far as Job knew, everything originated entirely with God, and he thus spoke of it.
Concerning his children and goods, he said, "The LORD gave
and the LORD has taken away; may the name of the LORD be
praised" (1:21). And as for the boils, he rebuked his wife with a
sublime declaration of trust: "Shall we accept good from God,
and not trouble?" (2:10).

Job was unaware of any secondary causes. He probably never
understood, in this life, what was going on in the cosmic realm.
Since he presumably knew nothing of Satan, he could not have
known that God was using him to prove to a cynical adversary
the possibility of authentic holiness. Satan had sneered at Job's
piety, claiming that it was only a front for selfish gain. "Every

man has his price," was his insinuation. But God said, "All right, I will show you one that hasn't."

But it had to be a "blind" test. Job was kept in the dark about God's "wager." He had no idea that God had a purpose and a reason for the terrible things that happened. Neither are we capable of understanding what is in God's mind—for our good and His glory—when He allows mysterious adversities and calamities to come into our lives.

So, "Does God cause everything that happens to me?" Yes and no. He is the ultimate cause of everything. He is not the immediate cause of everything, for several secondary causes exist in between. But in any case, God is deeply involved in everything that happens to His children. And He will have the last word. As this proved to be so with Job, so will this be so with us.

QUESTION: *In what way is God's providence most clearly seen?*

ANSWER: It is seen most dramatically in His management of circumstances. He opens and closes "doors"; He brings people and events together at critical times in their lives, with momentous, life-changing consequences.[1]

We see some simple but crucial examples in the life of Jesus. When Jesus wanted to enter Jerusalem at the beginning of Passion Week, He sent two of His disciples on a strange errand. "Go to the village ahead of you," He directed, "and at once you will find a donkey tied there, with her colt by her" (Matt. 21:2). The miracle was not just in Christ's knowledge of those circumstances but also in the divine providence that arranged them in advance, for that event began before Jesus got there. Perhaps this is what happened early that morning: The farmer said to his wife, "I need to go up to the city today to get a donkey-load of grain." She then suggested, "You won't need the colt, will you? Will you leave her behind?" The farmer hesitated, then said, "No, I have a feeling I should take her along. I don't know why." In this scenario God was putting this trip and these details into the farmer's mind because He wanted to fulfill prophecy that day. But this is the way God works—we call it providence.

Then there is what occurred later that week. When the disciples asked where Jesus wanted them to prepare for the Passover, He said, "As you enter the city, a man carrying a jar of water will meet you. Follow him to the house that he enters, and say to the owner of the house, 'The Teacher asks: Where is the guest room, where I may eat the Passover with my disciples?' He will show you a large upper room, all furnished" (Luke 22:10-12). Here is a remarkable sequence of events, far beyond the possibility of mere coincidence. The disciples got to the village at the same time as the man carrying the water. He was going to the right house. The owner understood who the Teacher was. The room was large, and it was already prepared. This is the way God can manage detail. It is not due to chance but providence.

QUESTION: *Is this how God brings about the fulfillment of prophecy?*

ANSWER: Yes. On a larger scale we see this divine managing of circumstances in the fulfilling of prophecy. God does this by moving the minds of people, controlling the weather, dovetailing the timing of events—all without robbing people of their free will at the basic level of their personal relationship with God. Witness the storm sent by God in the case of runaway Jonah. And look at Ezra's words: "In the first year of Cyrus king of Persia, in order to fulfill the word of the LORD spoken by Jeremiah, the LORD moved the heart of Cyrus king of Persia to make a proclamation" (Ezra 1:1)—a proclamation decreeing the rebuilding of the Temple in Jerusalem. God simultaneously worked not only on the king's mind but also on Ezra and "the family heads of Judah and Benjamin, and the priests and Levites —everyone whose heart God had moved" (v. 5). The Lord drew all these separate entities into a common force for the achievement of a divine objective.

QUESTION: *Can the circumstances leading up to and surrounding the birth of Jesus be seen as providential?*

ANSWER: Yes. These are by far the most astonishing centuries-long chain of events. They prepared not only Israel but also the world for the coming of Jesus. These seemingly small dots of decision and directional changes cascaded into a crescendo merging at Bethlehem that wonderful night we celebrate as Christmas Eve. The Roman Empire's vast road system, with its relative ease of travel; the empire's tax system and the emperor's decision to require registration and taxation at a person's place of origin; the availability of a humble cowshed; the end of a young woman's pregnancy; and a star that appeared to wise men in a faraway country—all were converging threads of history that became the means by which age-old prophecy was fulfilled.

QUESTION: *Can everything that happens to us be called providential?*

ANSWER: Everything is providential in the sense that God has provided all the materials of life right now—the air we breathe, food, shelter, family, friends, clothing, speech, even those who help the sick or handicapped. We live within His sheltering, protective wings.

Moreover, everything in our lives is providential in the sense that we are never absent to God, never forgotten by Him, never out of the circle of His care and concern. If He numbers the hairs of our heads, He is aware of our stomachaches, sore eyes, and moments of utter weariness.

Not everything that happens, however, is necessarily a special providence with a specific divine objective in mind. There is such a thing as chance—as, for instance, in a game of Scrabble, where we can hardly say that winning is a providential event. But the mystery of providence is that we never know what seemingly insignificant turn of events will prove to be critical in our lives and thus providential.

QUESTION: *Are some "bad" things sent purposely by God, not just "permitted"?*

ANSWER: Yes. God said to the Israelites, "Know then in your heart that as a man disciplines his son, so the LORD your God disciplines you" (Deut. 8:5). The discipline God had in mind here was the ruggedness of the previous 40 years, when life was not at all easy or pleasant. "He humbled you, causing you to hunger and then feeding you with manna, which neither you nor your fathers had known, to teach you that man does not live on bread alone but on every word that comes from the mouth of the LORD" (v. 3). God sent just enough hardness and difficulty to wean them from a total focus on the physical and to awaken within them some degree of spiritual understanding.

The New Testament picks this up and threads it into the economy of grace. In Heb. 12:1-14, the idea of purposeful trial is applied to our "struggle against sin"(v. 4): "Endure hardship as discipline; God is treating you as sons" (v. 7). What is the purpose of earthly fathers? To induce maturing and to produce good men and women. What is God's purpose? "That we may share in his holiness" (v. 10). Could any outcome be loftier than that? God really isn't interested in smoothing our path and humoring our whims, like an indulgent parent. He is interested in our character—not so much our happiness as our holiness. For holiness is the declared qualification for heaven (v. 14)—not happiness, prosperity, success, or even health.

QUESTION: *If God is not the only actor, what other forces or agents impact our lives?*

ANSWER: We can name Satan, the forces of nature, and humankind's own free will. There is no more important theological principle than that of secondary causes. God is not the only actor. There are other actors, and their effects are very real; in fact, their effects affect God himself.

We may say then that in the web of life the riddle of providence is the interweaving of God, Satan, natural law, the free actions of others, and the free actions of ourselves.

QUESTION: *What part does each play?*

ANSWER: That God is never absent, never indifferent, and never caught napping is a truism. He never throws up His hands in frustration, exclaiming, "What am I going to do now?" But is He in total and sole control of every event? If so, then Satan, natural law, others, and we ourselves are really not factors but only bit players in a rigged and predetermined charade.

If we grant any autonomy, or reality, at all to any agent or factor apart from God, then we must also acknowledge that God's agency in what happens is limited—a self-limitation but a true limitation nevertheless. Both this chapter and the previous chapter on divine sovereignty have made it clear that we have to choose between two options. There is either a real freedom given to moral agents, which makes true holiness possible, or a closed universe, which makes God as responsible for sin as He is for the movement of the stars. We cannot have it both ways.

QUESTION: *What part does Satan play in this drama?*

ANSWER: As we learned in chapter 3, he is the fountainhead of evil. In respect to providence, we need only to remember that he is a real person and has real power to intrude himself into human affairs. Paul told the Thessalonians that he wanted to return to them "again and again—but Satan stopped us" (1 Thess. 2:18). Astonishing! Here is Satan interfering with the flow of events in Paul's ministry.

QUESTION: *What about natural law?*

ANSWER: God created and set the natural order in motion. Furthermore, God upholds the natural order—"sustaining all things by his powerful word" (Heb. 1:3), but He seldom interrupts it. He enables it to function with both saint and sinner, "[causing] his sun to rise on the evil and the good, and [sending] rain on the righteous and the unrighteous" (Matt. 5:45). He also allows the law of gravitation to work equally with saint and sinner. The saint who falls out of a 10-story window will fall just as fast as will a sinner (although a *landing* miracle cannot be ruled out!).

Also, because of the curse (Gen. 3:17; Rom. 8:18-22) this natural order is disrupted with killer storms and earthquakes that strike God's people as well as the unsaved. At times God provides supernatural protection, that is, a miracle. But God does not promise to protect us always from natural forces, from the diseases that shadow a decaying humanity, or from accidents. Yet these are the forces that often affect us most profoundly and unpleasantly—and we are tempted to say, "Lord, why has this happened to me?"

Being children of God does not always shelter us from the common experiences of humanity. We live in a fallen world, and we suffer the same hazards as others. We don't blame God but Adam, and every generation since has copied Adam instead of turning to God.

God often heals—but He allows some of His children to die, even when it seems they are too young. God often protects—but He allows some of His children to be killed in accidents. We don't understand it, but we don't have to. Our privilege is to trust. That honors God far more than trusting only when we understand. And our steadfastness in adversity honors God far more than our "happiness" would if we were sheltered like hothouse plants.

QUESTION: *How important is the human will in all of this?*

ANSWER: It is more important by far than either Satan or natural law. The only force that can defeat God finally at the eternal level is a person's will to rebel. Although God can move our minds to do what He wants at the political or social levels of life and use us to bring about His purposes, He will not coerce us at the ultimate level to surrender to Him in repentance and faith for eternal salvation. He created that autonomy, and He will not violate it. When God created humankind in His own image, He took a great risk, for part of that image was the possession of free will.

QUESTION: *Are there differing views respecting this interplay between human freedom and divine action?*

ANSWER: Yes. There are whole theological systems that seek to

deny or at least hedge this freedom. They develop ways to say
that even what we think we do freely is really manipulated behind the scenes by God. This is called theological determinism.
According to this, just as a puppeteer's hands are hidden, so are
God's controlling hands.

We must reject this evasion and come to terms with the core
truth that freedom is real. The entire Bible everywhere assumes
that God interacts with human beings on the basis of a real freedom. All warnings, commandments, pleadings, condemnations,
and judgments testify that God is dealing with personal agents
who are capable, in total freedom, of disregarding the warnings,
disobeying the commands, and thus meriting the judgments. If
this freedom is not real, we are compelled to conclude (as irrever-
ent as it is!) that God's relation with humankind is playacting, and
any ultimate condemnation would be outrageously unjust.

Nothing is truer than the fact that human beings can thwart
God's plans and defy God's will. But also, their rebellion and
disobedience may ruin their lives and damn their souls. "Why
will you die, O house of Israel? For I take no pleasure in the
death of anyone, declares the Sovereign LORD. Repent and
live!" (Ezek. 18:31-32). This echoes the heartbroken call of God
to humankind from Genesis to Revelation.

QUESTION: *Can others hinder God's will for our lives?*

ANSWER: Definitely. God often overrules what He cannot rule
—as we shall see in a moment. But the human family is so inter-
related that we cannot escape the heartache nor the havoc
wrought by the sin of others. Ask any divorcé. Ask any child
whose daddy is in prison.

Is it necessary for victims of abuse, infidelity, or other broken
promises to say, "This must be God's will"? No, it is not God's
will; it is the will of Satan and wicked hearts.

Let's not try to force everything that happens into the category
of divine providence and sanctify it by dubbing it as God's will. It
has already been declared that sin is never God's will. If that is
true, then the direct effects of sin are not God's will either.

Here is a wonderful caveat, however: The sin of others cannot keep us out of heaven. It may influence us, confuse us, blight our lives, block the door of service, but it cannot neutralize the power of the Blood or blot out the loving face of God, if we but choose to keep our hand in His.

QUESTION: *Does God have a special promise covering the bad things that happen to us?*

ANSWER: Yes, Rom. 8:28: "And we know that in all things God works for the good of those who love him, who have been called according to his purpose." Let us be guided through the thickets by this assurance.

This passage does not say that God *causes* all things, but "in all things" God *works*. We have already seen that God can be said to be a cause of things if we think about what He permits and also about the kind of universe He has established. But He is not a cause in the sense that He decrees "all things" in advance so that they could not happen otherwise. And He is not the cause of all things in the sense that they are His primary will for us or that He engineered them.

QUESTION: *In what ways does God "work" for our "good"?*

ANSWER: By taking the entire mix of life and working within it to bring good out of it—not because of it—but in spite of it. God can overrule even when He cannot rule. Some things cannot be set right, for their die is cast—those murdered cannot be brought back to life, aborted babies cannot be found playing in a mother's kitchen, some broken marriages cannot be mended, squandered health cannot always be regained. But in spite of all this, if we truly repent and get back on the track of obedience, God can still salvage from the wreckage not only disciplined character but also renewed usefulness.

QUESTION: *Is there a catch?*

ANSWER: There is no catch but a condition. This promise is not just to anyone; it is to those who "love him, who have been

called according to his purpose" (Rom. 8:28). And what is His
purpose? It is "to be conformed to the likeness of his Son" (v. 29).

To "love him" means that we allow God to use the "all things"
toward the fulfilling of His purpose—our conformity to Christ.
This will rule out rebellion, unbelief, self-pity, and bitterness.

An acquaintance of mine packed a few things and walked
out on his shocked and grief-stricken wife, after 25 years of mar-
riage. He was gone for 2 years. They were divorced, and she got
the beautiful home.

During the 2 years, she had plenty of opportunities for dates,
but she refused, held steady, and prayed. She came to know God
in a depth and joy never dreamed of before. She became a
woman of spiritual radiance and power. God brought him back,
and they had 12 happy years before he died in faith. But the
point is not that they were reunited. It is that God "worked" in
this tragedy for "the good" of this woman, because she loved
Him enough to accept the good from His hand.

God did not turn the desertion and divorce into a good. It
was totally evil. Neither did God design the divorce to achieve
these lofty purposes. But God was able to *take* this tragedy and
control the outcome because He had a woman who loved Him
enough to put herself totally in His hands. The most wonderful
thing of all was that in the entire process this woman was being
"conformed to the likeness of his Son."

QUESTION: *Then can God take the evil deeds of sinful persons and turn them into "providences"?*

ANSWER: Yes. In the end this woman could look back on her experience and call it all "providential." It was providential because
she allowed God to make it such. The French saint Madame
Guyon, while a prisoner for her faith in Vincennes, 1698, could
write:

> *Oh, it is good to soar*
> *These bolts and bars above,*
> *To Him Whose purpose I adore,*
> *Whose providence I love;*

And in Thy mighty will to find
The joy, the freedom of the mind.[2]

Evil men put her in that prison. But because God had permitted it, Madame Guyon's love for God enabled her to embrace it and call it "providence." Likewise, the designs of Satan and wicked persons become providential to the trusting soul who keeps "looking unto Jesus" in all that happens and accepts it as being permitted with a loving design. Thus is Ps. 76:10 fulfilled: "Surely the wrath of man shall praise You" (NKJV).

QUESTION: *Are God's providential ways the same with outsiders as they are with His own people?*

ANSWER: No. God's providential management with those who love Him and put themselves into His hands as clay is different from His providential management in the lives of rebels, backsliders, or disobedient Christians. God loves to encompass those who keep in step with Him with providences of assistance, shelter, protection, guidance, and open doors.

This does not mean (as we have already seen) that God always exempts them from the normal hazards of life. But it means that even in adversity there is a sense that God has a steadying hand on events. How amazed we often are at the delicate timing and dovetailing of the circumstances in our lives.

But when we take ourselves out from under this umbrella of daily care, we find ourselves subject to a different kind of providence. We might call it the providence of *default*—the occurrence of a lot of negative things God probably would have protected us from if we had been in the center of His will. Then we may begin to suffer the providences of divine judgment, which our disobedience has prompted God to send into our lives.

At this stage these providences are disciplinary, having as their objective our recovery. But if these fail in His merciful purpose, the providences will cease to be in any measure from God but will be only the accumulating distresses of Satan and sin. Ultimate and final damnation will result from our "stubbornness and . . . unrepentant heart," which is "storing up wrath" against ourselves "for the day of God's wrath, when his righteous judgment will be revealed" (Rom. 2:5). These are the people to whom God finally will say, "Your will be done."

QUESTION: *What kind of providence is the most severe test to our faith?*

ANSWER: The severest test of our faith is the hurtful event God allows when we know He could have prevented it. God supernaturally delivered Peter out of Herod's hands but allowed Herod to kill James. Since God sent an angel to deliver Peter, we know He could have sent the same angel—or a thousand others—to save James. Do you suppose James's wife and family might have wondered?

A friend of mine was a theology professor. On his way home one dark night his little Volkswagen was hurled into the ditch by a hit-and-run vehicle. Both the car and my friend were broken and smashed. At that moment a medic drove by and noticed the mangled car. Normally, he said later, he never stopped for accidents on his way home; but this time a strange compulsion forced him to stop, give what first aid he could, and call an ambulance from his car phone. My friend's life was saved, but if the medic had not helped, death would have occurred in a few minutes, so severe were his injuries.

After my friend had spent months in the hospital, and after he had returned to the classroom, I said to him, "Wasn't it providential that the medic 'happened' along just at the right moment?" My friend was silent a moment, then pensively said, "Yes, but if God could do that, couldn't He just as easily have arranged for me to get to that corner five seconds later?" There you have it! That is the residual problem. The sending of the medic proved that God was involved. But God's allowing the accident to happen and not preventing it could only mean some mysterious purpose was hidden deep in God's sovereign wisdom.

After a few more years of teaching, my friend went to heaven. Do you suppose he looked up James and said, "Let's go ask the Lord why?"

I have a sneaking feeling that they never did. It was no longer a problem. Just being in Christ's presence would erase from their minds all unanswered earthbound questions. "What does it matter," they would say. "We're here!"

"Consider it pure joy, my brothers, whenever you face trials of many kinds, because you know that the testing of your faith develops perseverance. Perseverance must finish its work so that you may be mature and complete, not lacking anything" (James 1:2-4; cf. Rom. 5:3-4).

SIN
What Is Sin, and How Serious Is It?

QUESTION: *What is sin?*

ANSWER: Sin is anything that separates us from God and brings us under His judgment. If there were no God, the concept of sin would never arise. Society might have rules and punishments, perhaps calling violations crimes. But "sin" is a religious term and implies a willful breach with a holy God.

QUESTION: *Can we pinpoint the idea of sin more specifically?*

ANSWER: Yes. The idea of sin is very simple. God gave a command to our first parents, and they disobeyed. That is sin. Nothing could be easier to grasp than that. Now, thousands of years from Adam, we still have God's commands to deal with. The Bible is full of them. Disobedience to them is still sin. "The man who says, 'I know him,' but does not do what he commands is a liar, and the truth is not in him" (1 John 2:4).

QUESTION: *Did God give Adam and Eve a reason for the prohibition of a particular tree in the garden?*

ANSWER: No. The command symbolized God's authority and humanity's subjection to that authority. To have given a reason would have canceled the moral value of the test. An obedience based on implicit faith and entire surrender does not demand reasons. No explanation is needed beyond the simple fact of God's command. To insist on explanations in advance is to reserve the right of "line-item veto," which transfers ultimate authority from God to self. Even Jesus did not claim this right.

QUESTION: *Does this core sin—disobedience—imply related forms of sin?*

ANSWER: Yes. Related forms are *pride* and *unbelief.* When Adam and Eve accepted the possibility that God did not really mean what He said, they were experiencing doubt. Unless conquered, doubt soon becomes distrust, and distrust moves to unbelief.

Pride was generated by an awakening desire to be independent of God's orders. Satan promised them a level of power and knowledge God had not assigned to them. To overreach God's assignment and grasp for knowledge of "good and evil" equal to God's was pride in the following forms:

- It was a *rejection of God's declared boundaries* and hence a rejection of God's final authority. They were declaring their right to choose for themselves a role other than what God had given. This was rebellion. Sin always has in it a quality of rebellion.

- It was *a false confidence in their personal ability to determine right from wrong.* This is seen in Eve's bold scanning of the tree to see if she could detect anything wrong with it. When she found that it was "good for food and pleasant to the eye, and also desirable for gaining wisdom" (Gen. 3:6), she and, through her, Adam substituted their own evaluation for God's. They thus set aside not only God's specific word but also God's authority. They in effect implied that they did not need God and His rules. They could find their own way. This was pride in its most impudent form. Without realizing it, they were in effect transferring the mentoring role from God to Satan.

- It was *idolatry*, which is another name for the exaltation of self to the place of God. It was a declaration of personal autonomy—exactly as humans have been claiming for themselves ever since. They were rejecting God's primary claim on their lives.[1]

QUESTION: *What are the moral qualities of sin—without which an act may be a mistake but not sin (in the term's full sense)?*

ANSWER: This question can be answered by asking further questions. Did Adam and Eve know what the law was? *Yes.* Had they been clearly told what would happen if they disobeyed? *Yes.* Were they intelligent beings and therefore accountable? *Yes.* Were they free moral agents—able to obey or disobey? *Yes.* Then they were not forced by any outside agency to disobey, were they? *No.* Did they thus disobey in the possession of both knowledge and freedom? *Yes.*

When we put these ideas together, we get the essential meaning of sin as a moral term and as a moral event. People ignorant of the law cannot sin in this sense. Neither can people who have no freedom or ability to make moral choices. Thus people who are forced against their will to do wrong cannot be sinning. People with subnormal mental capacities cannot sin, because they are not accountable, and to hold them so would be unjust.

QUESTION: *Is it ever biblically proper to use the term "sin" when the essential moral element of blameworthiness is absent?*

ANSWER: Yes, because the Old Testament speaks of "sins of ignorance." This term referred to unknowing and unintentional transgressions of the cultic laws, such as touching a dead body or perhaps forgetting a prescribed sacrifice. It was never a term used to refer to "sins with a high hand," that is, conscious, deliberate wrongdoing. What's more, no harm existed until the inadvertent transgressor discovered what he or she had done or not done. Then the person would need to make atonement for the violation.

Clearly these laws distinguish between innocent mistakes and the guiltiness inherently belonging to sin "properly so-called" (Wesley). The problem is that both these types of behavior are called sins. This difficulty arises partly because the different Hebrew words designating these different levels of blameworthiness are all translated by the English word "sin." This throws us off and provides a foothold for the idea that we "sin in thought, word, and deed every day."

Having different levels of sin, then, is first of all a language problem. But more than that—it is also an emphasis problem. Because the old covenant was a covenant of written law buttressed by scores of secondary regulations, any violation, intended or not, was a deviation from perfection and needed setting right. In our day failing to see the posted speed limit absolves the driver of being a deliberate lawbreaker but does not cancel the bare fact of the violation and probably will not exempt the person from getting a ticket. The "sins of ignorance" in the Old Testament were something like that.

In the New Testament the emphasis has shifted from the letter of the law to the spirit of the law. This does not mean that the Old Testament was all law and no grace or that the opposite was true for the New Testament. But the emphasis did shift to seeing sin in strictly moral terms. This is why people living within the "sins of ignorance" framework are horrified at those professing they live above sin. In contrast, Christians living within the "sin as an act of willfulness" framework (as in 1 John) see that the avoidance of sin in the full moral sense is not only possible but also uncompromisingly expected. We can avoid much controversy and spiritual confusion if we clearly understand the difference between these two viewpoints.

Better yet, we will be truer to the tone of the New Testament if we learn to think strictly in moral terms. We should ascribe to "sin" the wickedness the term suggests and insist on its distinction from "sins of ignorance," which accrue no condemnation until discovered.[2] We should reserve what we agree is unavoidable to the category of mistake or infirmity, which because of its inner innocence does not break fellowship with God.

QUESTION: *Then does the concept of sin differ in the New Testament from what it is in the Old Testament?*

ANSWER: Yes. In a legal order, any infraction of a law, whether intentional or not, is called sin. But in the New Testament the emphasis is shifted to the fundamental concept of sin as a moral event. A moral event is similar to the original sin in the Garden of Eden—a deliberate disobedience, involving knowledge of the law, freedom to choose, and evil intention.

QUESTION: *How much leeway should we give in granting patience with unintended faults and failings?*

ANSWER: As much as we want others to give us. Our humanity, even sanctified humanity, is comprised of human finiteness *plus* the scars and weaknesses from being maimed in the Fall. But these scars and weaknesses are in themselves innocent, since they are the unavoidable legacy of our ancestry. For example, a "drug baby" addicted at birth because of its mother's habits cannot be blamed for sin, only pitied. If Adam had made a mistake in naming the animals, would he have been condemned and driven from the garden? No, he was driven from the garden, not for any mistakes, but for deliberate disobedience.

QUESTION: *Are there other reasons why some Christians believe sin to be unavoidable?*

ANSWER: Yes. Not only do people confuse sin with mistakes, but also they confuse sin with temptation. The Bible makes it clear that temptation to sin does not become sin until yielded to (1 Cor. 10:13; James 1:15). Even Jesus was tempted but did not sin.

People also confuse sin with the natural appetites. Some urges are biological in nature, not always sinful. A flash of sexual interest in another person may merely be the agitation of properly functioning glands. But God expects us to control these urges and keep them within His declared boundaries. If we assume that every urge needing to be controlled is itself sin, then we will have a continually uneasy conscience and may start believing sin to be inevitable.

QUESTION: *Is continued sinning (in the proper moral sense) compatible with the Christian life?*

ANSWER: It is not only incompatible but *ruled out*. When the Bible deals with sin as a moral event, for which we are fully responsible, it excludes sinning from Christian living. There is zero tolerance—though always with the possibility of forgiveness on the terms of 1 John 1:9. This same zero tolerance is equally in the Old Testament when sinning with a "high hand" is in mind. "The soul who sins is the one who will die" (Ezek. 18:20).

Here are a few stinging verdicts on sinning found in the New Testament: "Everyone who sins is a slave to sin" (John 8:34). Obedience to sin spells being "slaves to sin, which leads to death" (Rom. 6:16). "The wages of sin is death" (v. 23). "Make not provision for the flesh, to fulfil the lusts thereof" (13:14, KJV). "I write this to you so that you will not sin" (1 John 2:1). "No one who lives in him keeps on sinning. No one who continues to sin has either seen him or known him" (3:6).

And as if these verses are not enough, the final blow to a "sinning saints" theology is this: "Dear children, do not let anyone lead you astray. He who does what is right is righteous, just as he is righteous. He who does what is sinful is of the devil, because the devil has been sinning from the beginning. . . . No one who is born of God will continue to sin, because God's seed remains in him; he cannot go on sinning, because he has been born of God" (1 John 3:7-9).

QUESTION: *What are the implications of these verses?*

ANSWER: First, sin has immediate spiritual consequences: *It separates us from a holy and loving God.* In the words of Randall K. Hartman: "A consequence of sin in our lives is that God always reacts negatively to it. He cannot tolerate it. It sickens Him. He would not be a holy God if He did not respond in such a manner to sin."[3]

QUESTION: *What other unmistakable teachings are implied?*

ANSWER: The following are clear enough:

- Living in Christ and living in sin at the same time are impossible. They are mutually exclusive.
- Those who are continuing to sin are still under the control of the devil.
- Those who consciously make allowance for the practice of

sin have not thoroughly repented. We cannot be one person inside and another outside.

- Teachers who seek to harmonize sinning with the Christian life are false teachers. They are leading others "astray."
- Quite obviously what the inspired writer means by "sin" is something far more serious than mistakes and shortcomings.

QUESTION: *Then does the New Testament concept of sin in terms of heart attitude and intention make victory over sin easier?*

ANSWER: In one way, yes, for it clears the air of false guilt and needless condemnation. But in another way, no, for sin is now seen more as happening on the inside than the outside. In God's sight internal hatred is akin to murder and a lustful look is adultery committed in the heart.

Sin as a moral concept is further intensified when it is seen as a violation of the most important law of all—the law of love. This forces upon us the sobering awareness that sinning is not just an act of legal wrongdoing but *a failing to love.* It is a failing to keep God's two commandments to love—to love Him and to love our neighbor. Since Jesus called these two commandments the greatest, in fact the lynchpin of all the others, then no matter how legally correct a person's life may be, if that person does not love, he or she is guilty of the worst sin possible.

QUESTION: *How serious, then, is sin (defined in its full moral sense)?*

ANSWER: The gravity of sin is incalculable. The potential devastation of one sin is beyond measure. Like a stone dropped in a pond whose ripples spread to the farthest shores in every direction, so a single act of sin, in its widespread influence, can have effects that can never be reversed throughout all eternity. How can any punishment equal the ill caused by even one sin that is eternal in its consequences? Sin therefore creates eternal guilt and blameworthiness.

When we think of the awful truth that people may be eternally in hell because of our sins—our bad example, our unkindness, our neglect, our unfairness, our words—we reel at the sheer horror of such responsibility. We begin to realize that there is no way to undo the awful effects of *our* sins. If not for God's incredible mercy, the immeasurable guilt would not only drive us mad but also sink us into hell along with those whose damnation our sins have contributed to.

QUESTION: *In addition to creating guilt and separating us from God, what effect does sinning have on our own nature?*

ANSWER: It compounds the depravity, or corruption, we inherited from Adam. Adam's sin began this corrupting process, and we willfully continue it. We are cursed by a change in what drives our very being, and this makes it easier to sin than not to sin, to rebel than to obey, to doubt than to believe, to be unholy than to be holy. Adam's primitive nature was Godward driven; human nature after being blighted by Adam's sin is selfward driven. We call this original sin, and it infects the moral and spiritual nature of every person who comes into the world. When we reach the age of accountability and allow this nature to rule us by deliberately sinning, we add our own corruption to Adam's and compound both our depravity and our guilt.

QUESTION: *How total can our depravity become?*

ANSWER: We are faced with the awful, terrifying truth that sin can so corrupt our very nature that our moral death becomes irreversible. Our spiritual death can become so complete that we can lose all memory of goodness, all capacity to love purely, and all interest in holiness. The ultimate result of sin is a corruption as absolute as the devil's. Any first step of rebellion away from God starts a person down this terrible path and has within it the seeds of this awful, irrevocable destiny.

It is frightfully clear that humanity is in a hopeless state and, apart from the intervention of a merciful and holy God, is inescapably doomed. But the Good News is that we have a Deliverer, who can not only set us free from sin's grip but also reverse sin's effects. Christ can make us holy in the sight of a holy God and make us fit for a holy heaven.

THE ATONEMENT
Why Did Jesus Die?

QUESTION: *Does the Bible tell us why Jesus came into the world?*

ANSWER: Yes, very precisely. "Here is a trustworthy saying that deserves full acceptance: Christ Jesus came into the world to save sinners" (1 Tim. 1:15). Christ modeled what normal humanity is like. He taught us what God the Father is like and how to relate to Him in prayer. He explained how we should live. He demonstrated compassion by feeding the hungry and healing the sick. But none of this reached the heart of Jesus' real mission—which was to save sinners.

QUESTION: *Save them from what?*

ANSWER: From sin, the fundamental problem, and from hell, the end result of sin. What separates us from God is not poverty, ignorance, infirmity, or the mistakes and limitations these handicaps produce. It is sin and sins. This focus of Christ's coming is revealed in His name: "You are to give him the name Jesus, because he will save his people from their sins" (Matt. 1:21). As others have often declared, "Jesus did not die to save people *in* their sins but *from* them."

QUESTION: *How is this salvation related to Jesus' death?*

ANSWER: His death on the Cross makes this salvation possible. Various attempts have been made to explain how this can be so. We call them theories of the Atonement. They include the following:

The Ransom Theory. This holds that in His death Christ was paying a demanded ransom to Satan, thus winning humanity's release.

The Christus Victor Motif. This sees Christ's death as winning through His voluntary sacrifice and resurrection a victory over Satan, which makes possible our personal deliverance from the world, the flesh, and the devil.

The Moral Influence Theory. This sees Christ's death as only a demonstration of the love of God, the objective of which is to woo sinners to repentance and allegiance.

The Penal Satisfaction Theory. This stresses the legal consequences of sin and the necessity of paying on behalf of humanity the penalty announced by God in the Garden of Eden: "When you eat of it you will surely die" (i.e., die spiritually; Gen 2:17).

The Governmental Theory. According to this theory Christ's death was necessary as a means of fulfilling the obligation of good government.

There are several other theories, but this is not the place to dissect them. Each one makes some contribution to our total understanding.

QUESTION: *Can we establish a baseline in our understanding of the Atonement?*

ANSWER: Yes. We are on sure ground when we say His death was *substitutionary*, which means He died in the sinner's place. It was a *penal* death—death as a penalty. In the Crucifixion we see what is essential to understanding His death, that is, His identification with the two thieves and with the curse of the law (Gal. 3:13). He died the death we deserved. He took upon himself the guilt of our sins and paid the penalty on our behalf so that God might have a moral basis for freeing us from that penalty. God's own integrity was at stake. He had pronounced the penalty of death for sin. To keep His word, either the sinner must die or a substitute must die. Jesus voluntarily became that substitute. By believing in this sacrifice on our behalf we are discharged from the personal penalty of our own sins and declared *righteous*. This is *justification* (Rom. 5:1).[1]

QUESTION: *How does the Bible explain Jesus' death?*

ANSWER: The Bible is very clear. Speaking of Jesus, Paul says, "God presented him as a sacrifice of atonement. . . . He did this to demonstrate his justice . . . so as to be just and the one who justifies those who have faith in Jesus" (Rom. 3:25-26). God's justice is satisfied by the death of His Son, which means His mercy may be extended to the sinner without violating His justice. To ignore sin would be wrong. God's holiness prohibited any kind of mercy that would even have the appearance of being soft on sin.

Yet we must avoid caricaturing Christ as merciful and the Father as harsh. The Atonement was the work of the Father as well as the Son, for it was God the Father who "so loved the world that he gave his one and only Son, that whoever believes in him shall not perish but have eternal life" (John 3:16). The Holy Spirit was equally involved, for it was "through the eternal Spirit" that Jesus "offered himself unblemished to God" (Heb. 9:14). The Atonement was the gift of the Triune God.

Christ's death was on our behalf because it was the death we deserved to die. In so offering himself as the sacrificial Lamb, Christ was not overcoming a divine reluctance but removing a moral obstacle. The divine holiness required the imposition of the declared sanction against sin, but to save us God allowed the death of His Son to satisfy that demand. There was no other way to reconcile mercy and justice. If there had been, the Triune God would have taken it. To suppose this way of making salvation possible was unnecessary is to fail to grasp the enormity of sin, on the one hand, and the profundity of God's holiness, on the other. God's holiness makes forgiveness without atonement impossible.

QUESTION: *Is it vital to our Christian faith to maintain an emphasis on the blood of Christ?*

ANSWER: Yes. What is crucial to our understanding is not simply that Christ died but that He shed His blood as a sacrificial lamb. "Look," exclaimed John the Baptist, pointing to Jesus, "the Lamb of God, who takes away the sin of the world" (John 1:29). The word "blood" signified a kind of death that was *capital*, that is, one that paid the death penalty. The writer to the Hebrews reminds us that Jesus in making atonement did not enter the "Most Holy Place" by "the blood of goats and calves; but he entered . . . by his own blood, having obtained eternal redemption" (Heb. 9:12).

And although the blood of animals provided a temporary covering for sin under the old covenant plan, "How much more, then, will the blood of Christ, who through the eternal Spirit offered himself unblemished to God, cleanse our consciences from acts that lead to death, so that we may serve the living God!" (v. 14).

The stress placed in the New Testament on the blood of Christ is so central that instead of being squeamish about the word "blood" in our songs and sermons, we should allow the word to fill us with reverence, humility, and intense gratitude. At the same time we can understand the natural aversion of the unregenerate, who in his or her blinded state is completely unable to comprehend this stress on blood as something beautiful instead of merely gory.

QUESTION: *Did Christ die for all or only for the "elect"?*

ANSWER: John 3:16 answers that question: "For God so loved the world that he gave his one and only Son, that whoever believes in him shall not perish but have eternal life." The "world" includes all human beings who have ever lived, who live now, and who will live in the future. One limitation only is declared—the benefit of Christ's death is promised solely to those who believe.

The "whoever" is not determined in advance by God's decree. The plain meaning of the verse is the exact opposite. Every person has the option to believe and can choose to do so if he or she will. This is an honest "whoever." God has no secret agenda for "fixing" the promise to certain persons He selects. Any opinion otherwise is to charge God with insincerity and trickery.

QUESTION: *Did Jesus accomplish our salvation by dying for us?*

ANSWER: In one sense, yes. He brought all of humankind into the sphere of grace. Even though all persons come into the world with a sinful nature, they also come into the world justified. It is this universal justification that assures the salvation of those who die in infancy. But because all commit sin when they reach the age of moral responsibility, it is necessary for each one to claim this provided justification for himself or herself. This is what we do when we repent and believe in Jesus for our personal salvation. The situation is like a generous bequest for an entire community, but individual participation must be claimed voluntarily, one by one.

Thus while in one sense Christ accomplished salvation for humankind, in another sense He only provided a grace status, which the individual must endorse and make his or her own.

QUESTION: *How does this differ from Calvinism?*

ANSWER: Those who believe in an irresistible divine sovereignty—Calvinists—also believe that God's control is so total that all effects of the Atonement are divinely fixed and predetermined before the creation and even before the Fall. Christ's death was thus a transaction between the Father and Son that unconditionally secured the salvation of the elect (those chosen to be saved). If we are among the elect, then we were saved when Christ died, our new birth being only our discovery of our predetermined saved state. In this case, such a fixed salvation cannot be lost—hence the belief in unconditional eternal security.

However, the Bible everywhere presents the Atonement as Christ's provision and God's invitation, not an irresistible accomplishment at the personal level. The sinner's response to

Christ's death on the Cross is presented as an option, not as a predetermined outcome. Sinners are offered salvation, a salvation they may reject and are always in danger of rejecting. "Repent," "Believe," "Obey," "Persevere," "Lay aside every weight," "Pray," "Ask," "Do not harden your hearts," "Do not resist the Spirit"—these are the exhortations that structure the tone of the Word of God.

When Paul preached at Athens, he assured the crowd that God now "commands all people everywhere to repent" (Acts 17:30). The command to all is evidence that all can repent, and that God wants them to repent because He wants to save them—no exceptions. If He commands all to repent but does not intend to save all who repent, He is mocking them, and the very hint that our great God would so trifle is sheer blasphemy.

Even moderate Calvinists these days are going all out to repudiate the doctrine of a limited atonement and are arguing for the good news that Christ's death was for all. Norman Geisler is one such Calvinist who sees clearly the difference between a substitutionary atonement that purchases an unrefusable salvation and one that provides full access to salvation without compelling the intended beneficiary to take it. He says, "Of course, if substitution is automatic, then everyone for whom Christ is substituted will automatically be saved. But substitution need not be automatic; a penalty can be paid without it automatically taking effect."[2]

Even though Jesus by His death provided adequate grace for all, there is something we must do to close the circuit. The electric power company has made available all the current we could possibly need, but it will run no machinery, light no rooms, and provide no heat until we get connected with the system. Likewise, it is necessary for you and me, as individuals, to come to Christ in repentance and faith.

QUESTION: *Are there any benefits from the Atonement that are automatic, which we experience before we are actually "saved"?*

ANSWER: Yes. These come under the general name "prevenient grace"—the grace that "goes before." Prevenient grace is a universal benefit of the Atonement that the Holy Spirit applies to every member of Adam's race. This grace has several facets:

- It makes us *salvable,* that is, capable of being saved. No one is so corrupt that he or she is outside the circle of God's grace or beyond the reach of the Holy Spirit. The exception is the fully accountable adult who by deliberate and continued rejection of the Holy Spirit commits spiritual suicide—even before he or she dies physically (see Matt. 12:31-32).
- Prevenient grace, released by the Atonement, enables us to make a free choice. The doctrine of total depravity teaches that our depravity is such a complete loss of moral ability and spiritual inclination Godward that if left to ourselves we would have neither the ability nor the desire to be holy or to love and serve God. But prevenient grace sensitizes the human heart to the convicting influences of the Holy Spirit; but beyond this, it restores our ability to make a truly free moral choice in respect to God.
- The Atonement covers infants and all defective human beings, who because of their handicaps are irresponsible. Speaking of infants, A. T. Robertson says, "The sinful nature which they inherit is met by Christ's atoning death and grace."[3]
- Prevenient grace is a *restraining grace* (sometimes called "common grace"). Until this restraining influence is so resisted that God gives people "over to a depraved mind" (Rom. 1:28), it will hold them back from many evil deeds and preserve a measure of common decency. As corrupt as the world is, it would be a lot worse if the Spirit were not at work among people. To the extent that the Spirit withdraws, to that extent will the prophecy of 2 Tim. 3:1 be ful-

filled: "But mark this: There will be terrible times in the last days."

- Prevenient grace is the universal ministry of the Holy Spirit in every human heart, urging to better things, creating hunger for God and righteousness, stirring up uneasiness, gripping the conscience with a sense of guilt and shame, and convicting of sin. This is what Jesus had in mind when He said the Holy Spirit "will convict the world of guilt in regard to sin and righteousness and judgment" (John 16:8). Arnold Hodgin visited at one period of his life a hundred mission stations around the world and talked with hundreds of nationals. He said to this writer that he became convinced there was no person who did not at some point in his or her life experience a powerful sense of conviction for sin.

QUESTION: *What are the benefits of the Atonement that we experience when we are saved?*

ANSWER: A partial list can be seen in Rom. 5:9-11: "Since we have now been justified by his blood, how much more shall we be saved from God's wrath through him! For if, when we were God's enemies, we were reconciled to him through the death of his Son, how much more, having been reconciled, shall we be saved through his life! Not only is this so, but we also rejoice in God through our Lord Jesus Christ, through whom we have now received reconciliation."

At conversion, the primary benefit is *justification* (v. 9). This is pardon for our sins—being released from their condemnation. In our justification we also find *reconciliation* (v. 10). We are "set right" with God. We sometimes say, "I wonder if he [or she] is right with God." And we urge people who are ill to "make their peace with God." We mean that they need to become "justified" and "reconciled" to God. The enmity is dissolved and the separation ended. "Therefore, since we have been justified through faith, we have peace with God through our Lord Jesus Christ" (v. 1).

When we experience justification, we know what it means to "rejoice in God through our Lord Jesus Christ, through whom we have now received reconciliation" (v. 11). We have known fear and dread but not joy. Because of what Christ's death has won for us, we enter into a new relationship with God as Father, Friend, Comforter, Guide, Provider.

QUESTION: *Are there other benefits of the Atonement?*

ANSWER: Yes. There is not only justification but also regeneration, by which we are raised spiritually from death to life and given a new nature. There is adoption into the family of God. There is also sanctification, by which the sinful nature of our birth heritage is corrected and our nature brought back to a state of natural attraction to God. While justification is a change in status, sanctification is a change in state.[4]

The means of our regeneration is the action within us of the Holy Spirit, and the means of our sanctification is the infilling of the Spirit in the full Pentecostal grace of purity and power. We enjoy the indwelling Spirit's comforting presence and fellowship; divine guidance and protection; grace for the trials of life; healing of our bodies as God wills; molding us into strong Christlikeness; usefulness in advancing Christ's kingdom; and finally, if we stay on course, gift to us of heaven. "He who was seated on the throne said, 'I am making everything new!'" (Rev. 21:5). And this same Person promised, "He who overcomes will inherit all this, and I will be his God and he will be my son" (v. 7).

Even while God was creating the earth He was saying " I AM creating all this to be over-seen by a holy Adam."

HOLINESS
How Can I Be Holy?

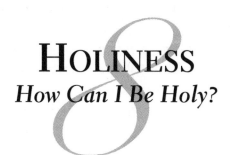

QUESTION: *How important is holiness in the plan of salvation?*

ANSWER: It is the core of God's redemptive plan for humankind. Holiness was what we lost in Adam and is what God designed for us to recover in Christ. "For he chose us in him [Christ] before the creation of the world to be holy and blameless in his sight" (Eph. 1:4). Adam's sin and its devastating effect on us does not change God's will that we be holy; it just means that now holiness is possible only through Christ.

QUESTION: *But is not being "saved" more important than being holy?*

ANSWER: No, for the two cannot be separated. Salvation from hell in the next life depends on our being saved from sin in this life, and being saved from sin is being made holy. Eph. 1:4 does not say that God chose us in Christ to be *saved* but to be *holy*.

Although salvation in heaven is the *ultimate* goal, holiness is the *immediate* end. And if the latter is not reached, the former will never be reached. "Without holiness no one will see the Lord" is God's decree (Heb. 12:14). "Everyone who has this hope in him [of seeing the Lord] purifies himself, just as he is pure" (1 John 3:3). "Nothing impure [unholy] will ever enter it [the Holy City], nor will anyone who does what is shameful or deceitful" (Rev. 21:27).

"The destined end of man," writes Oswald Chambers, "is not happiness, not health, but holiness. . . . The one thing that matters is whether a man will accept the God who will make him holy."[1]

QUESTION: *Exactly what is this "holiness" that was lost in the Fall (the sinning of Adam)? Why is its recovery essential to salvation?*

ANSWER: It is a right disposition *toward* God and a personal, lively relationship *with* God. Humanity was created with a spiritual nature that was inclined toward God. This means a natural attraction existed between God and humanity. But holiness included not just a natural attraction but also a one-to-one fellowship. We cannot be "holy" apart from this living, here-and-now communion with God. By definition holiness consists of *both* a God-inclined nature and a dynamic personal relationship.

When Adam sinned, the living fellowship *and* the holy disposition were lost. The disposition became an inclination to run from God instead of running to Him, while the fellowship was replaced by alienation, even hostility. The recovery of this lost disposition and unmarred fellowship is the holiness God has planned for us in Christ. Suddenly such words as "awakening," "repentance," "forgiveness," "regeneration," "cleansing," "purity," "separation," and "sanctification" become crucial to the human situation.

Being made holy is being "conformed to the likeness of his Son" (Rom. 8:29). God would rather have us be like Jesus than have us be healthy, successful, or even happy. And un-Christlikeness would make us gross misfits in heaven.

QUESTION: *Was anything else lost in the Fall?*

ANSWER: Yes. Physical health and clarity of mind were lost in the Fall. These losses were natural effects of Adam's sin. Stemming from these losses came disease, deformity, ignorance, annoying limitations, and frustrating infirmities. These forms of decadence are not a part of what is called original sin, but secondary side effects. The recovery of holiness is the recovery of a right disposition and a living, unmarred fellowship with God; it is not the immediate elimination of these side effects. Salvation from these is included in God's total plan but not fully available in this life.

QUESTION: *If holiness as right disposition and recovered fel-lowship is so central in God's plan, what should be our atti-tude toward holiness?*

ANSWER: Our attitude should be to prize holiness as God does. If God's purpose for us in Christ is for us to *be* holy, *being* holy should be our purpose also. In fact, our spontaneous response to the subject of holiness is the exact reflection of our *real* attitude toward God. A professed love for God is contradicted by an in-ner resentment toward the teaching of holiness. Oswald Cham-bers says that the stirring up of "petulance" in us by the preach-ing of Bible truth is proof that we "are yet carnal."[2]

QUESTION: *Are there other verses that declare this recovery of holiness to be central to God's plan for us?*

ANSWER: There are many, but here are two: 2 Thess. 2:13 and 1 Pet. 1:2. The Thessalonian declaration is, "God from the begin-ning chose you for salvation through sanctification by the Spirit" (NKJV).[3] According to the verse in 1 Peter, God's elect "have been chosen according to the foreknowledge of God the Father, through the sanctifying work of the Spirit." In agreement with Eph. 1:4 both of these verses trace God's will that we be holy to His original precreation plan. They give us an added note of in-formation—while Christ is the Source of our holiness, the Holy Spirit is the sanctifying Agent; that is, in these verses "through" means "by means of."

Also the Word says that the "wisdom from God" (the whole redemption plan) consists of "righteousness, holiness and re-demption" (1 Cor. 1:30). Here are the three branches of our full salvation, neither one of which is dispensable. When churches talk a lot about righteousness (justification by faith) and future resurrection but say little or nothing about holiness, we know they have a truncated gospel.

QUESTION: *What is the preferred rendering of Eph. 1:4?*

ANSWER: It is better to follow the NKJV, which keeps "in love" with the preceding words, instead of breaking the clause with a period and putting "in love" with the next verse, as is done by the NIV. This would make the end of the verse read, "We should be holy and without blame before Him in love" (NKJV).

QUESTION: *Does this help us better understand what is meant by the word "holy"?*

ANSWER: Yes. The word "holy" can stand alone in the sense of (1) separation to God, (2) setting apart for holy use (consecration), and (3) purity from sin. However, the added phrase "in love" adds to our understanding of "holy" by conforming the idea more fully to the New Testament concept of holiness as perfect love. Holiness is not only cleansing, purity, and separation but also wholehearted dedication and devotion. It is loving God with "all [the] heart . . . soul . . . mind and . . . strength" (Mark 12:30). The true nature of holiness is a love for God that puts Him first in all things. This is essential to recovering the holiness lost in the Fall.

QUESTION: *Is the word "blameless" significant?*

ANSWER: Very. This helps us distinguish between holiness as perfection in love and holiness as absolute flawlessness.[4] The question of "blamelessness" versus "blameworthiness" is one of *motives* (why we do things) and *intentions* (what our aims are). God accepts us as holy if He sees that our love is governed by right motives and right intentions. Why did I give that thousand dollars? To be considered generous? What was my secret intention? To gain some personal advantage? To obligate God to prosper me? To salve my conscience? Or was it the glad expression of a real passion for souls and a transparent love for Christ?

We need to see that love is the only element of the Christian life in which perfection is possible. Because of those side effects of the Fall (remember?) that remain with us all through life, we cannot be perfect in performance. Our inadequate knowledge, poor judgment, and many infirmities (such as nervous tension) prevent such perfection. But we can love God and people blamelessly. We can love God with all our heart, soul, mind, and strength—free from unbelief, divided loyalties, lukewarmness, and rebellion. Our love for people can be free from indifference, ill will, an unforgiving spirit, covetousness, and duplicity. We can be free from pretense. "Love must be sincere" (Rom. 12:9; cf. 2 Cor. 6:6). The sincerity of our love is revealed by our godly hatred of "what is evil" and our consistent clinging to "what is good" (Rom. 12:9).

If there is secret sin in our inclinations and motives, we are not blameless but blameworthy. To the extent that our heart is divided, lukewarm in our devotion to God, or deceitful in our relations with people, to that extent we are unholy.

QUESTION: *How can we illustrate the difference between blamelessness and flawlessness?*

ANSWER: Children often need to be taught and corrected when "blaming" in the sense of condemning would be inappropriate. A three-year-old kept pulling his grandfather's kale plants up. After the third time, he was spanked. Years later his mother asked him if he remembered the event. When he said yes, she asked why he did it. "I thought I was helping Grandpa," he explained. "I had seen him pull up stuff, so I thought those plants needed pulling too." He was faulty but not blameworthy.

When Paul prays that the Thessalonians be sanctified "wholly" (1 Thess. 5:23, KJV) and that they be thereafter "preserved," he is not praying that they will be kept flawless but "blameless." Fortunately, while we are often blamed by men (maybe even spanked by misunderstanding parents!), only God's evaluation is always correct, and in the long run only His really matters.

QUESTION: *With this distinction in mind, is it correct to say that biblical holiness is "wholeness"?*

ANSWER: Not unless we add "spiritual" to "wholeness." Complete personal wholeness would include the whole person—body, soul, and spirit. Although this whole person is to be sanctified—made holy—this is not the same as being made totally well. There need be no sin, but there still may be sickness. A sanctified body is not necessarily a well body. A sanctified mind is not necessarily a well mind. Some forms of mental illness are forms of real physical illness and need medical care just as surely as an infected appendix. This can be as true of wholly sanctified people as it can be of carnal or unregenerate people.

It has often been said that what physical health is to the body, and sanity is to the mind, so holiness is to the soul. This means holiness is normalcy, just as physical health is normalcy and sanity is normalcy. But we can have one without the others. Total "wholeness" would be a threefold healthiness. But while Christian holiness is the enjoyment of spiritual health and freedom from sin, this holiness can exist without the corresponding normalcy in the other two areas.

QUESTION: *Is it possible even on the spiritual level to be truly holy but not yet wholly holy?*

ANSWER: Yes, all "double-minded" believers (James 4:8) are truly holy yet not entirely holy—or "wholly holy." This was true of the Thessalonians, otherwise Paul would not have prayed that they be sanctified "completely" (1 Thess. 5:23, NKJV; "through and through," NIV). Implied in this prayer is a degree or kind of holiness that is already experienced.

QUESTION: *In what ways are born-again Christians already holy?*

ANSWER: They are holy in at least four ways:

1. Their lifestyle is consistently religious. The church is the center of their lives. They seek out the fellowship of God's people. Their lives in the home and away from home are marked by prayer, Bible reading, and worship. The traditional word for this is "piety."

2. Their conduct is righteous. "As obedient children, do not conform to the evil desires you had when you lived in ignorance," admonishes Peter. "But just as he who called you is holy, so be holy in all you do" (1 Pet. 1:14-15). In our relationships at home, in the community, in the church, and

in business, we are to be honest, fair, and dependable. Not
only so but also we are to be pure—faithful to our spouses,
prudent with the opposite sex, clean in our stories.

3. The born-again Christian is holy in the sense of "initial
   sanctification," which means that this Christian lets the
   Spirit clean him or her up. True repentance renounces
   the continued practice of known sin and deliberately
   seeks to form new and holy habits. The Corinthians, even
   though "carnal," were nevertheless holy in this sense.
   When Paul lists the common evil practices of that day, he
   reminds them, "And that is what some of you were."
   Then he rejoices with them: "But you were washed, you
   were sanctified, you were justified in the name of the
   Lord Jesus Christ and by the Spirit of our God" (1 Cor.
   6:11). The sanctification referred to here is *initial* sanctification, which essentially is cleansing from habitual pre-
   conversion filth and from the acquired depravity resulting
   from a person's own life of sinning. ("Acquired" differenti-
   ates this type of depravity from the "inherited" kind.)

4. The born-again person is also holy *positionally.* This is
   another aspect of the kind of holiness Paul ascribed to the
   Corinthians (the same people whom he later calls "carnal"!), when he addressed them as "those sanctified in
   Christ Jesus and called to be holy" (1 Cor. 1:2). Positionally they were sacred because of their relationship to
   Christ. Their standing before God was acceptable, because their faith in Christ was "credited" to them as righteousness (Rom. 4:23-24).

Because of this positional holiness they would have gone to
heaven if they had died within the hour. But if they lived, they
would come under the second part of the clause: "and called to
be holy" (1 Cor. 1:2). What they were positionally, they were expected to become practically. Sanctity must be supported by
saintliness.

Because positional holiness implies God's ownership, it carries a serious ethical claim. Just as people desecrate a church

building by allowing it to become filthy, so a Christian desecrates Christ and the name "Christian" by living a life that does not exhibit true, consistent Christ-honoring saintliness.

QUESTION: *In what way is the holiness of the "born-again" incomplete?*

ANSWER: The holiness that marks every true Christian is incomplete because to maintain it the Christian must struggle with a foot-dragging in his or her own nature. The inherited desire to be his or her "own person" still lurks within. As a result, very subtle conflicts of will arise frequently, sometimes resulting in sin. Rom. 7 vividly describes this struggle, and in crises of will the "dwelling in me sin" shows itself to be very powerful. Crucifixion with Christ is not yet as real to this person experientially as it ought to be and can be. The command "purify your hearts, you double-minded" (James 4:8) is relevant here.

QUESTION: *What are the marks of this incompleteness?*

ANSWER: The same marks we find in the disciples before Pentecost: spiritual thickheadedness, frequent displays of a worldly viewpoint, a strong inner response to fleshly appeals and values, divided motives, selfish ambition, rivalry with each other. These are also the same marks we find in the Corinthians: divisiveness, jealousy and envy, and pride. Their values were askew. Spiritual gifts were prized more than love and harmony.

To these traits we can add a tendency to rebel in the clutch; to grumble at God; to be censorious; to hold grudges and bitterness; to be self-seeking; to have embarrassing outbursts of temper; to have too many and too frequent defeats; and, in such ways, to fall shamefully short of Christlikeness and personal ideals. A true born-again believer who struggles with these carnal wobblings is greatly disturbed about them; often resolves to do better; strives in his or her own strength; and, because of repeated failures, is even at times tempted to give up. But this very struggle is what drives this believer in true brokenness back to the Cross.

QUESTION: *What is the answer?*

ANSWER: A second work of grace. We call it entire sanctification. We also call it the baptism with the Holy Spirit. It is what transformed the disciples on the Day of Pentecost. Immediately after the Resurrection Peter was rescued from his backsliding, but he was not cured of what caused it until filled with the Spirit.

This special sanctifying act of the Holy Spirit is necessary because the deep inclination toward self-willfulness is not a deed needing to be forgiven but a condition of the heart needing to be cleansed. Just as God forgives sins when the sinner sees them and repents of them, so God will cleanse believers when they see what Wesley called "the ground of their heart," become fully aware of the problem, and are fully willing to surrender totally to be cured.[5]

QUESTION: *But do we not "surrender" to the Lord when converted?*

ANSWER: Yes, but the surrender is much like the surrender of a rebel to a ruler. A person "gives in" to Christ as Lord and Savior because that person wants to be relieved of the burden of his or her sins. Such a person is not so much a soldier asking for orders as a renegade pleading for mercy. He or she wants the peace Christ offers but does not realize that this surrender is actually very narrow and superficial. It does not reach the depths of his or her impulse to claim the right to self-ownership.

In the days following conversion the natural tendency is to suppose that we still belong to ourselves and can live pretty much our own lives—though of course now basically righteous lives and certainly religious lives. The only things needing change, we assume, are the evil practices. When we have gotten rid of these, we can continue to live our everyday lives virtually as we please. Buying and selling, making a living, marrying and raising children, friendship, recreation and hobbies—all are activities of our own choosing. Concerning them we think we are expected to be "on our own."

But sooner or later God will jolt us with the awakening that

He wants much more than we have given, at a much deeper level. The carnal mind will fuss about this new aspect of stewardship. But the Holy Spirit will stop at nothing less than total capitulation and total consecration. What is more, the Spirit wants to burn out all fussing and so change our very nature that we will be *happy* to bring all of life under God's complete control.

The *total surrender* described in Rom. 6:13 and Rom. 12:1 must now be made. It must be made deliberately, profoundly, irrevocably, unconditionally, and also intelligently—for a person needs to survey the ground and become thoroughly aware of what this total surrender means, not only at the moment but also in the future. It will touch everything and may revise everything it touches. Associations, vocation, finances, family, ambition, recreation, entertainment—all of these will come under sharper control by the Spirit than ever before. Our hunger for full holiness must be so deep that we completely abandon ourselves to God, with a total willingness to obey absolutely and pay any price for the sanctifying fullness of the Holy Spirit in our hearts.

It took 10 days of group prayer to get the disciples ready for whatever the Lord had for them when the Day of Pentecost came. It may take some honest digging and seeking for us to get to that place. When we know we are there, we walk into the experience simply by claiming it, in the name of Jesus. For it is by faith that we lay hold of the power of the Blood and the certainty of the promises for our full sanctification.

"Everyone who has this faith," writes John Wesley, "purifies himself even as He is pure, purifies himself from every earthly, sensual desire, from all vile and inordinate affections, and from the whole of that carnal mind that is enmity against God."[6]

Let us say then that entire sanctification is the cleansing of the carnal mind by the infilling of the Holy Spirit and the establishment of God's love as the ruling temper and motivation of life. It is true all Christians have the Holy Spirit in His regenerating and directing office. However, entire sanctification requires the conscious enthronement of the Holy Spirit, as the deputy of Christ and the Father, in the whole of everyday life—

not only in keeping us on the road to heaven but also in perfecting our stewardship en route.

QUESTION: *But Wesley talks about our purifying ourselves. How can this be reconciled with Paul's prayer in 1 Thess. 5:23 that God does the sanctifying?*

ANSWER: It is true that such passages as 2 Cor. 7:1, James 4:8, and 1 John 3:3 make us responsible for our own purifying. These verses stress what we can and must do. We can confess our condition. We can consecrate fully. We can obey Rom. 6:13 and 12:1-2. We can surrender every lingering poison of ill will and every point of controversy with God. We can pray, tarry, seek, claim the promises, and exercise faith. In other words, we can be totally and aggressively involved in the sanctifying process, rather than dawdle in lazy passivity. But in the end, the cleansing beyond our reach, deep down in our inner nature, is the work of the Holy Spirit.[7]

QUESTION: *Does this work of grace solve every problem?*

ANSWER: No, it neither solves every problem nor meets every need. As Oswald Chambers says, "Deliverance from sin is not deliverance from human nature."[8] It is not deliverance from a lifetime of wrong opinions either.

But it is the indispensable foundation for such solutions and supplies for meeting needs. Peter *still* had to learn God's will for the Gentiles; but without the heart cleansing of Pentecost he would have been much harder to teach. In fact, without Pentecost it is unlikely he would have been fasting and praying on that rooftop in Joppa at all.

QUESTION: *Will Christians be lost who cannot testify to a second work of grace?*

ANSWER: Not if they are walking in the light according to 1 John 1:7. The holiness essential for seeing the Lord (Heb. 12:14) is a state of rightness with God right now. The five wise virgins

(Matt. 25:1-13) were welcomed into the wedding because their lamps were trimmed and burning when the bridegroom arrived. While no sinfulness of heart will enter heaven, hearts of sincere, obedient believers who have not yet reached a second crisis will be graciously cleansed at the moment of death. Those who are in spiritual jeopardy are Christians who have seen their inner need, have felt God's convicting call to full holiness, and have rejected it. Such persons forfeit their justification by their disobedience. Their destiny will match the five foolish virgins who supposed they wouldn't need the extra oil and were shut out. We must conclude that the least acceptable level of holiness is eagerness for the most available. But such eagerness is demonstrated by the promptness of our seeking "the full measure of the blessing of Christ" (Rom. 15:29) and submitting to the blessing of Paul's prayer (Eph. 3:14-21) that the Spirit so strengthen us with power "that Christ may dwell in [be in charge of] your hearts through faith" (v. 17).

FAITH
What Does It Mean to Be Saved by Faith?

QUESTION: *What is faith?*

ANSWER: It is belief in someone or something. Faith in a person is belief that he or she is trustworthy. Faith in a report is belief that the report is true. Faith in God is a firm belief that God exists. But that is the lowest rung of faith. Deists believe that God exists, but that is as close to God as they get. The faith God looks for is believing not only that He exists but also that "He is a rewarder of those who diligently seek Him" (Heb. 11:6, NKJV).

This means that if approaching God is going to be successful, we must approach in faith, not in unbelief. Unbelief cannot please God because it reflects a distrust of God. We either doubt His existence or doubt His power or distrust His goodness. Our Heavenly Father can no more be pleased when we distrust Him than an earthly father would be pleased if his child said to him, "Dad, you're OK, I guess, but I really don't trust you."

QUESTION: *How does faith differ from hope?*

ANSWER: Faith related to God and spiritual realities is "being sure of what we hope for and certain of what we do not see" (Heb. 11:1). Faith differs from hope in the sense that what we hope for is not yet experienced. It is out ahead. But faith is an inner assurance or certainty that our hope is justified.

QUESTION: *Then does faith differ from sight?*

ANSWER: Yes. I cannot believe for what I have in my hand. I can only be thankful for it and proceed to use it. But, "We live by faith, not by sight" (2 Cor. 5:7). Thomas insisted on sight. "Unless I see," he declared, "I will not believe." Christ humored him, and Thomas exclaimed, "My Lord and my God!" But Jesus said, "Because you have seen Me, you have believed. Blessed are those who have not seen and yet have believed" (John 20:24-29, NKJV).

QUESTION: *How does faith differ from credulity?*

ANSWER: Credulity is willingness to believe without a reasonable ground for belief. Credulous people believe too quickly. They are swayed by "every wind of doctrine" that sweeps their way. Biblical faith is not wishful thinking. It is not believing "what we know ain't so," as the little boy said. It is rather a logical deduction that reasons, "Because I know this to be true, it is reasonable to believe that what this points to is true." Bursting buds in the spring make it logical for me to believe that summer is coming.

QUESTION: *Then should we find fault with Thomas because he insisted on evidence?*

ANSWER: Everyone should have logical reasons for what he or she believes. The problem with Thomas was his unwillingness to accept the testimony of eyewitnesses. His fellow disciples reported to him that they had seen the living Lord. For Thomas to reject their testimony was to say, in effect, that they were either liars or fools. He knew them too well for that. So he should have believed them, as an expression of faith in the word of intelligent and honest persons.

QUESTION: *What then did Jesus mean when He said,
"Blessed are those who have not seen and yet have believed"
(John 20:29, NKJV)?*

ANSWER: Jesus knew that soon He would be leaving them, and
the kind of sight demanded by Thomas would be unavailable
until the Second Coming (or until death). Jesus was implying
that all Christians who came after Thomas would have to believe without sight. But He was saying that they would be as
blessed as those who had seen Jesus personally. That is, they
would be as sure as Thomas was, because their faith would be
based on the Word and the inward confirmation of the Holy
Spirit. That kind of certainty would be available to everyone
everywhere in every age.

QUESTION: *Does this mean that all Christian faith now be-
gins with faith in the Word?*

ANSWER: Exactly. There can be no valid faith in Jesus unless we
have faith in the Bible as the Word of God. And our faith in the
Bible is based on the supernatural credentials of its history, its
fulfilled prophecies, its own claim to divine inspiration, the obvious trust put in it by Jesus himself, and most of all the fact that
the New Testament events were reported by eyewitnesses. The
whole issue thus boils down to our ability or inability to believe
Matthew, Mark, Luke, John, Paul, Peter, and others as honest,
intelligent, and reliable reporters. If these persons were untrust-
worthy, then the foundation under the whole Christian edifice is
destroyed, and the building falls to the ground. In that case, let
us all get our hats and go home—and mourn.

QUESTION: *Does this not imply that prime importance must
be attached to our concept of the Scriptures?*

ANSWER: Yes. It is not without good reason that thoughtful
scholars perceive that when faith in the Bible falters, Christen-
dom, in all its branches, is adrift. Tradition and secular history
are inadequate to sustain a viable Christian faith.

QUESTION: *Are there Bible passages that show how belief in the Bible is foundational to belief in other doctrines?*

ANSWER: Yes. Our faith in creation, for instance, is derived from faith in the Bible. "By faith we understand that the universe was formed at God's command, so that what is seen was not made out of what was visible" (Heb. 11:3). It is the Bible that teaches us this. By believing the Scriptures we come to this understanding.

Even more relevant to the question is Rom. 10:17: "So then faith comes by hearing, and hearing by the word of God" (NKJV). Here is a very basic principle that applies equally not simply to the gospel but also to any other idea that asks for our faith. Faith cannot arise in an intellectual vacuum. Attempting to believe in a mystical, undifferentiated "idea blob" is nothing but superstition. But when a proposition is presented to the mind, the mind has a concept it will accept as true, doubt as uncertain, or reject as a falsehood. When the mind becomes reasonably convinced the proposition is true, faith on the intellectual level has been born. Such faith becomes strong and is properly consummated when it acts in accordance with what it has perceived to be the truth.

QUESTION: *Is this the way saving faith arises?*

ANSWER: Yes. It is only when we hear the gospel that our minds have something to take hold of. There is something about the power of the gospel, enabled by the Holy Spirit, which, to produce faith, needs only sufficient exposure. People with an open mind who keep hearing Bible preaching and in addition keep reading the Scriptures will either gradually or suddenly become aware that *this is the truth.*

They may not act on the truth, and as a consequence their faith may not become saving faith; in fact, in stubbornness they may refuse to acknowledge the truth and may continue to masquerade as unbelievers. But a truth discovery has happened from which they will never quite escape, and they will face this discovery at the Judgment.

QUESTION: *Is faith totally unrelated to sight?*

ANSWER: No. As we walk with God, the future is unseen and the vast kingdom of God in the invisible world is not open to our inspection. In this sense, walking by faith is the opposite of walking by sight. But in reality all faith walking is also sight walking. This startling statement, so apparently contradictory, needs some careful explanation.

The Bible is the history of God's self-revelation, all of which was visible and audible. Humanity's five senses were active in perceiving the truth of God. The Garden of Eden was a very visible and physical place. God's voice was audible, and His pronouncements were unmistakable. The Israelites saw the fire and smoke at Mount Sinai and heard God's thunder. They saw the sign of God's presence in the smoke that guided them by day and the pillar of fire at night. The "manna" was physical stuff they could pick up, cook, and eat.

When God the Son came, He was fondled by Mary, seen by shepherds and wise men, followed visually by disciples, and heard audibly. Five thousand people who tasted, chewed, and swallowed fish and bread out on the hillside could never be persuaded it was just an illusion. When Jesus arose, He was seen that very Sunday by many and then by some 500 people at once, claims Paul. His Ascension was visible and physical. The outpouring of the Holy Spirit on the Day of Pentecost was very physical: the crowd was drawn by the sound of the wind, their attention was captivated by the unlearned languages, they heard Peter's voice explain what had happened, and their baptism was in real water.

And so we could go on. But what is the meaning of all this? Simply that this self-revelation of God and this coming of His Son consisted of a long series of real events that was captured by the inspiring Holy Spirit in words written down and kept for all ages. In the pages of the Bible these events live again. The Holy Spirit makes them real to us, in all their inspiring, revealing, convicting, and instructing power. Christian faith is believing the truthfulness of this Record. This means that Christian faith is *seeing* for ourselves all of these events through the eyes of Moses,

Samuel, David, Matthew, John, and all the Spirit-enabled re-
corders. They become real to us by reliving them in our imagina-
tions and refeeling them in the devotion of our hearts. Thus faith
hears Jesus say to us what He said to the leper wanting Him to
cleanse him: "I am willing. . . . Be clean!" (Matt. 8:3). In one
sense, then, faith is living without sight; but in this very deep and
elemental sense, faith is living by sight. But the first necessity of
this sight is seeing the Bible as the Word of God.

QUESTION: *Does strong faith depend on seeing miracles?*

ANSWER: No. Strong faith does not ask for the props of additional miracles, because it rests on the "visual" evidences found in
the Bible. The rich man in hell (Luke 16:27-31) begged Abraham to send Lazarus back to his five brothers. When Abraham
reminded him that his brothers already "have Moses and the
Prophets," he protested, "No, father Abraham . . . but if someone from the dead goes to them, they will repent." The answer
was, "If they do not listen to Moses and the Prophets, they will
not be convinced even if someone rises from the dead."

Jesus knew perfectly well the stubborn, unruly nature of human sinfulness that does not want to believe. Honest, sincere
seekers after the truth will find in the Scriptures more than
enough evidence to convince them if they are willing to be convinced. If they are not willing, the multiplying of miracles will
make no difference. When Lazarus was raised from the dead,
the chief priests and the Pharisees, instead of believing, went into a frenzy and called together the whole Sanhedrin to plot his
death! (See John 12:9-10.) And today "signs and wonders" may
draw crowds but will not convert sinners, as long as the sinners
love their sins and will not give them up.[1]

QUESTION: *Exactly what is the place of faith in the plan of
salvation?*

ANSWER: Faith is a kind of believing that accepts as true the
gospel and relates personally and trustingly to Jesus Christ as
Savior. There are four actions in it:

1. It is a discovery of the mind by which we perceive the gospel to be true—that Jesus Christ really *is* the Son of God, that He really *did* die for our sins, that He really *did* rise from the grave, and that He really *is* alive today and wants to relate to us personally and knowingly.
2. It is this mental belief in basic Christian propositions being translated into earnest prayer, in which we confess our sins, forsake them, and plead for forgiveness in the name of Jesus.
3. It is a deliberate receiving of forgiveness and a placing of our full trust in Jesus. When this is sincere, our faith is confirmed by the inner witness of the Holy Spirit, which turns faith into assurance.
4. It is an act by which we identify ourselves with Jesus and acknowledge Him openly as our Savior.

In all these points of faith, faith's strength determines exactly what we get from God. Jesus declared this principle to the two blind men. "Do you believe that I am able to do this?" He asked. When they replied "Yes, Lord," He promptly declared this principle: "According to your faith will it be done to you" (Matt. 9:27-29). Little faith will receive little. Much faith will receive much.

QUESTION: *Is faith a faculty, like our reason, or is it a gift, like a family heirloom?*

ANSWER: It is both. As a faculty we exercise faith every day, when we send a letter, write a check, or drive a car. But this is a faculty we must learn to exercise wisely, lest it become gullibility. It is easy for us in our simplicity, especially when we are young, to be "taken in."

Nevertheless, this is the kind of faith faculty that can be turned toward Christ, and in this case it is optional for us. When the Philippian jailer cried out, "Sirs, what must I do to be saved?" Paul and Silas instructed, "Believe in the Lord Jesus, and you will be saved" (Acts 16:30-31). Paul and Silas apparently saw believing as something this man could choose to do.

Yet it was a gift too. As the jailer opened his heart to the truth, the certainty of it flooded in. Throughout the night as he listened to Paul's explanation of the gospel, his faith grew stronger and more sure every minute. When he was baptized, he was rejoicing. We can say that while his ability to believe was a natural faculty and his ability to exercise it toward Christ was a gift of prevenient grace, his believing was voluntary.

In Philippi, "The Lord opened [Lydia's] heart to respond to Paul's message" (Acts 16:14). She was inclined and willing to be receptive, or she would not have been at that prayer meeting. But the Lord, moving on her hungry heart, quickly convinced her that these men were telling the truth.

QUESTION: *Doesn't Eph. 2:8 say that our faith is the gift of God?*

ANSWER: No. The verse reads, "For it is by grace you have been saved, through faith—and this not from yourselves, it is the gift of God." Greek scholars know that the antecedent of "gift" is not "faith" but the *salvation* we receive through faith.[2]

Many of us are like the demon-possessed child's father, who had to cry out, "I do believe; help me overcome my unbelief!" (Mark 9:24). We choose to exercise our faith faculty, but as we do, the Spirit encourages and reinforces us. This continues until faith becomes a restful assurance that that for which we believe will become personal experience. Faith is strong enough to dis-place anxiety.

QUESTION: *Is saving and sanctifying faith what Paul means by the gift of faith listed in 1 Cor. 12:7-13?*

ANSWER: No. Saving faith is the faculty of faith being directed toward a personal trust in Jesus, because at some point our mind has perceived the truth, and we grasp it for ourselves. The "faith" listed by Paul as one of the gifts is special in the same way the other gifts are special—they are given to different individuals by the Holy Spirit, "just as he determines" (v. 11). These are service gifts, not grace gifts. These cannot be our gifts by our choice or by our efforts at development. They are given to us, one gift to one person and another to another person, according to God's wise sovereignty.

Paul remarks that "a faith that can move mountains" is utterly futile without love (1 Cor. 13:2). This suggests that the faith listed among those in chapter 12 is a special largeness of daring faith that can believe for large accomplishments and actually see them come to pass.

QUESTION: *Can this "gift of faith" be also a faculty that can be developed?*

ANSWER: Yes. The line is very fine between possessing this kind of faith as a supernatural, instantaneous gift and possessing such faith as a spiritual faculty that has become strong because of much use. George Mueller's faith was an example of a kind of faith that was both a gift and a faculty. Undoubtedly his years of exercising his faith had developed it to an amazing degree. He learned to pray and believe for the daily supply of all that was needed for the operation of his orphanages. By the time he was an old man, it could be claimed that he had *believed in* supplies for the education, clothing, housing, and feeding of 10,000 orphans. But he began timidly and gingerly, with a small faith that persisted, and as he saw God work in answer to simple prayer and faith, his faith matured and could claim more and more.

QUESTION: *How is faith related to works?*

ANSWER: Closely—but in a rather complicated way. If we think clearly and study the Bible carefully, we will come up with three propositions—all true:

Faith excludes works.
Faith depends on works.
Faith produces works.

QUESTION: *In what sense does faith exclude works?*

ANSWER: Let us refer again to Eph. 2:8. This means that neither our faith nor our own efforts are the source of our salvation; God alone is. God has taken the initiative. He saves us "through" faith, that is, using our faith as a catalyst, but not because of our faith. The "because" must be traced to John 3:16: "For God so loved the world that he gave his one and only Son . . ."

Not only is faith simply the catalyst, but also Paul immediately adds the words "not by works, so that no one can boast" (Eph. 2:9). By this he means that our salvation is not *earned* or *achieved* by anything we can do. A young person who desires a certain academic degree earns it by enrolling in a specific program of studies and by pursuing the program to its satisfactory completion. When this person is awarded the degree, it can be said that he or she *achieved* it. But the experiencing of salvation is not like this. No amount of law keeping or good deeds can earn enough "brownie points" with God to cancel our sins and secure for us a home in heaven. Salvation has been made possible by the blood of Christ as a totally free gift, which requires only our sincere faith to receive it. As the Reformers insisted, it is *sola fide*—"faith alone." The moment we start trusting our own righteousness, we block the working of grace.

QUESTION: *Then how can we say that faith depends on works?*

ANSWER: By examining the word "sincere" in the last paragraph. What is faith reaching for? It is reaching for forgiveness of our sins, our adoption into the family of God, and an assurance of eternal life. To desire these blessings *sincerely* requires that we confess our sins with true sorrow and turn from them wholeheartedly. To desire to become the children of God means that in all earnestness we want to be godly. To sincerely want eternal life means much more than simply wanting to escape hell; it means we want to fulfill the whole destiny of humankind, which, as the Westminster Shorter Catechism says, is "to glorify God and to enjoy him forever." But without the kind of faith that wants holiness, we will neither glorify God nor enjoy Him forever. Heaven would be pure misery for a human being with an unrepentant heart full of sin and corruption.

Thus saving faith *depends* on the "work" of repentance. And this is exactly what the Bible teaches. "Produce fruit [evidence] in keeping with repentance," John the Baptist thundered to the Pharisees and Sadducees (Matt. 3:8). Paul's preaching was structured by the insistence that having saving faith in "our Lord Jesus" must be based on first turning to God "in repentance" (Acts 20:21). Before King Agrippa, Paul even ascribed the priority of repentance to the words of the Lord Jesus himself, who personally commissioned Paul to preach so that sinners might "turn . . . from darkness to light, and from the power of Satan to God" (26:18). This is exactly the kind of preaching Paul engaged in: "I preached that they should repent and turn to God and prove their repentance by their deeds" (v. 20). Here is faith that is *dependent on works*.

To repeat, these are not works of merit by which salvation is earned, but works of sincerity that are essential to the moral nature of turning to God. Calvin has been credited with saying that salvation is by "faith alone, but the faith that saves is not alone." Faith that tries to be alone, without repentance and obedience, is a sham before people and a scam attempted on God.

QUESTION: *How can it be said that faith "produces works"?*

ANSWER: Works make faith complete. They prove faith and fulfill its purpose and meaning. This can be illustrated in many ways. A man might believe ever so strongly that this bus about to stop at this corner is able to carry him as a passenger, but this level of faith will do him no good unless he gets on. His getting on perfects and proves his professed faith. The money we have in the bank is the practical proof of our faith in the bank. If I truly believe the doctor, I will take the medicine.

Of course it is possible that people may genuinely be convinced that something is true, trustworthy, and important, yet they stubbornly refuse to make use of it themselves. The would-be passenger may choose to remain standing at the corner. The bank believer may still keep his or her money at home. The patient may declare roundly his or her faith in the doctor, yet throw the medicine down the toilet and die. The so-called faith in each case is abortive, and if the sinner acts that way toward God, the sinner's intellectual faith will never get him or her to heaven.

Clearly the fundamental work faith produces and keeps on producing as long as the faith remains "sincere" (1 Tim. 1:5) is the work of obedience. Disobedience, or any form of conscience violation, will make "shipwreck" of faith (v. 19). Paul in his warning to Timothy refers to two persons by name who apparently were the first "unconditional eternal security" people—Hymenaeus and Alexander. They supposed they could compromise the faith and tamper with their conscience without losing saving faith. Paul's revulsion and rejection of this presumption was so severe that he "handed [them] over to Satan to be taught not to blaspheme" (1 Tim. 1:18-20).

QUESTION: *How does this faith principle relate to love?*

ANSWER: While the principle of faith producing works is applied biblically in numerous ways, it is most significantly associated with love. "What good is it, my brothers," queries James, "if a man claims to have faith but has no deeds? Can such faith save him? Suppose a brother or sister is without clothes and daily food. If one of you says to him, 'Go, I wish you well; keep warm and well fed,' but does nothing about his physical needs, what good is it? In the same way, faith by itself, if it is not accompanied by action, is dead" (James 2:14-17). John applies the same truth to love in 1 John 3:17-22. This blending of faith and love will create hearts that are "eager to do what is good" (Titus 2:14).

It is clearly fundamental to a biblical understanding of faith that we grasp its relation to works. If we do, we will see that the propositions that faith excludes works, faith depends on works, and faith produces works are all true.

QUESTION: *Among the various Christian doctrines is there one that above all needs to be believed with unshakable conviction?*

ANSWER: Yes—the Resurrection. This is the bellwether. "In times like these you need an anchor," the song says. The fact of the resurrection of Jesus Christ is that anchor, for it validates everything else. If we doubt the Resurrection, we will have no basis for holding on to any other Christian claim. The raising of Jesus from the dead is our assurance that His death was a true atonement rather than merely a martyrdom. It proves His identity as the Son of God. It vindicates His announced mission, "to seek and to save what was lost" (Luke 19:10). It confirms His power to perform the miracles the Gospels record. It explains the events of Pentecost and how the writers of the New Testament were able to recall His words and proclaim a gospel of power with utter confidence.

Faith in the Resurrection is our sure grounding in our personal storms. We ask at times for miracles of healing, but we do not receive them. We pray for our children, but they are still out of the fold. We experience blow after blow of life's harshness, and at times it seems as if God is uncaring. But if in the very center of our confusion and perplexity we have the solid anchor of knowing that Jesus is alive, we can hold steady in the buffetings of life—even joyfully. For the Resurrection means He hears prayer. It means that all of His teachings and claims are true. It means we can count on Him to keep His word. It means that by His Spirit He is with us in our sorrows and griefs—we are not alone. It means that the future is as bright as His promises. If we are sure of the Resurrection, we can be sure that we are on the winning side; that Satan is headed for the bottomless pit; that Jesus has gone to prepare a wonderful place for us; and that as He promised, He will come again to receive us to himself to be with Him forever. With this certainty written deep in our very being, we can overcome anything. We can survive pain, lost jobs, outrageous fortune, disappointments, loneliness, ostracism, poverty, misunderstanding, and lingering disease. We know who holds our hand, and we know what is ahead.

If our confidence is dependent upon answered prayers, bodily healings, successful ventures, unlimited prosperity, and freedom from pain, then we will be unsure, wobbly, anxious, fretful, and fearful all our lives. But if we are grounded on the sure fact of the Resurrection, we will "be steadfast, immovable, always abounding in the work of the Lord, knowing that [our] labor is not in vain in the Lord" (1 Cor. 15:58, NKJV).

NOTES

Preface

1. Rosamond Kent Sprague, ed., *A Matter of Eternity: Selections from the Writings of Dorothy L. Sayers* (Grand Rapids: William B. Eerdmans Publishing Company, 1973), 32.

Chapter 1

1. See Ralph Earle's *How We Got Our Bible*, rev. ed. (Kansas City: Beacon Hill Press of Kansas City, 1992) for the history of the formation of the canon—the list of books recognized by the Church as inspired Scripture.

2. Erwin W. Lutzer, *Seven Reasons Why You Can Trust the Bible* (Chicago: Moody Press, 1998), 125.

3. Gerhard Maier, *Biblical Hermeneutics*, trans. Robert W. Yarbrough (Wheaton, Ill.: Crossway Books, 1994), 175.

4. Concerning the possible alternate reading of 2 Tim. 3:16, "all Scripture inspired of God" (instead of "all Scripture is inspired"), James Orr says that this "may be a broader, but it is certain that it is not intended to be a *narrower*, form of statement than the other. The apostle assuredly does not mean to draw a distinction between a Scripture which is inspired and a Scripture which is not inspired, or to suggest that any of the 'sacred writings' of the previous verse fall into the latter category. Such an idea is totally foreign to his thought" (*Revelation and Inspiration* [1910; reprint, Grand Rapids: Baker Book House, 1969], 161).

5. Many misinformed people automatically associate the term "verbal inspiration" with dictation. This is unfortunate. Many of the greatest Evangelical scholars subscribe to the verbal inspiration approach but vigorously disavow the notion of dictation. What they mean by "verbal" is at least similar if not identical to what H. Orton Wiley meant by the "dynamic theory" of inspiration.

6. H. Orton Wiley is equally misunderstood. While he espoused the dynamic theory, what he had in mind was by no means loose and porous. "By inspiration," he writes, "we mean the actuating energy of the Holy Spirit by which holy men were qualified to receive religious truth and to communicate it to others without error" (*Christian Theology*, vol. 1 [Kansas City: Nazarene Publishing House, 1941], 168; cf. 175). Communicating "without error" would be possible only if the "actuating energy of the Holy Spirit" went farther than simply putting thoughts into the minds of the writers.

7. Orr, *Revelation and Inspiration*, 159.

8. Heard on the radio program *Discover the Word*, produced by RBC Ministries, Grand Rapids, broadcast over KGNW, 10 October 2000.

9. Maier, *Biblical Hermeneutics*, 177.

Chapter 2

1. Michael J. Behe, *Darwin's Black Box* (New York: Simon and Schuster, 1996).

2. This poses a problem for our conception of God as a person. Here are three Persons; how can three Persons be one Person? We can only see this by understanding that the term "person" in relation to the Trinity carries a specialized, technical meaning, as an entity within the one Person, God. They are not persons as three unrelated people whom we meet on the street are persons. Each divine Person shares equally yet uniquely in this unitary Personhood.

3. Gerald Bray, *The Doctrine of God* (Downers Grove, Ill.: InterVarsity Press, 1993), 192, 203. Bray ascribes this position to Augustine.

4. Wiley, *Christian Theology*, vol. 2, 148. Wiley also speaks of the Incarnation as an "indissoluble union" (159).

5. Ibid., 172.

6. The "no other name" stipulation rules out the names of Muhammad, Confucius, Buddha, or any other god or leader. Any conscious salvation in this life must be through believing in Jesus when Jesus is presented to the mind and conscience. There is some hint in the New Testament that sincerely repentant pagans, earnestly seeking after a true God, will be covered on the basis of what God sees they would do if the gospel reached them. This seems to be the import of Rom. 2:4-11. The provision is universal, for Christ died for all. Those who have heard the gospel and rejected it have no reasonable ground for hope. But those who are seeking and die without having yet heard will know within moments after death that their salvation was purchased by the blood of Jesus Christ. So it is still "no other name."

Chapter 3

1. D. M. Lloyd-Jones, *What Is an Evangelical?* (Carlisle, Pa.: Banner of Truth Trust, 1992), 81.

2. "Satan" means adversary; "devil" or "the devil" is from the Greek *diabolos* and means slanderer, accuser. *Baker's Pocket Dictionary of Religious Terms* says, "The Talmud and the Scriptures regard him as having been a mighty angel who fell from heaven through pride and rebellion" (Donald T. Kauffman, ed. [Grand Rapids: Baker Book House, 1967], 383.

3. In Ezek. 14:14-20 God identifies Job as a historical person along with Noah and Daniel.

4. Norman Geisler, *Chosen but Free: A Balanced View of Divine Election* (Minneapolis: Bethany House Publishers, 1999), 22.

5. The premise in John Milton's epic poem *Paradise Lost* is that the fall of

Satan could have been analogous to Nebuchadnezzar's pride and ambition, whom Isaiah called "O morning star, son of the dawn" (Isa. 14:12-15).

6. C. S. Lewis, *The Screwtape Letters*, in *The Best of C. S. Lewis* (New York: Iversen Associates, 1969), 69.

Chapter 4

1. Clark Pinnock observes, "The all-powerful God delegates power to the creature, making himself vulnerable. In giving us dominion over the earth, God shares power with the creature. The fact of sin in history reveals the adverse effect that disobedience has on God's purpose" (*Openness of God* [Downers Grove, Ill.: InterVarsity Press, 1994], 115).

2. C. S. Lewis observes that if God intervened every time people were abusing their free will "so that a wooden beam would be soft as grass when it was used as a weapon," freedom of the will would be void (quoted in Walter Hooper, *C. S. Lewis: A Companion and Guide* [San Francisco: HarperSanFrancisco, 1996], 298).

3. C. S. Lewis, *The Great Divorce*, in *The Best of C. S. Lewis* (New York: Iversen Associates, 1969).

4. G. Campbell Morgan, "The Government of God," in *26 Sermons by G. Campbell Morgan*, The Evangelical Reprint Library, vol. 1 (Joplin, Mo.: College Press, 1969), 58.

5. What about the declarations in the Bible of God's hating Esau and hardening "whom he wants to harden" (Rom. 9:12-13, 18)? This discussion is within the context of God's sovereign use of means and agents, and terms such as "hate" and "harden" must be understood in that light. "Hate" means to reject from first place, and "harden" means to confirm people in their rebellion so as to use their rebellion as an instrument—as in the case of Pharaoh. But in the light of John 3:16, we can no more interpret God's hating Esau as personal dislike than we can interpret Jesus as meaning dislike and dishonor when He declares, "If anyone comes to me and does not hate his father and mother . . . he cannot be my disciple" (Luke 14:26). In both cases, the sense of rejecting from first place is consistent with both God's love and His claims. Also we must interpret "harden" in the light of Rom. 11:32-33. For further discussion see my treatment of this in *God, Man, and Salvation* (Kansas City: Beacon Hill Press of Kansas City, 1977), 430-38.

Chapter 5

1. See 2 Kings 8:1-6 for an amazing example of the providential converging of circumstances.

2. Jeanne Marie Bouvier de La Motte Guyon, *Sweet Smelling Myrrh: The Autobiography of Madame Guyon*, ed. Abbie C. Morrow (Salem, Ohio: Schmul Publishing Company, 1996), 192.

Chapter 6

1. Commenting on David's declaration in Ps. 51 that his sin against Bathsheba and Uriah was primarily against God, Charles W. Carter says, "He is forthrightly admitting that since God is the creator of all, any offense against God's creation is primarily an offense to God himself, who created all, and whose it is." A further explanation is "accounted for by the fact that man bears the image of God. Therefore any sin is a violation of that sacred image. . . . Sin mars God's image in man, and that is an offense against the One whose image is represented in humanity" ("Hamartiology," in *A Contemporary Wesleyan Theology*, vol. 1 [Grand Rapids: Francis Asbury Press, 1983], 247).

2. For further discussion of sins of ignorance, see my article "The Question of 'Sins of Ignorance' in Relation to Wesley's Definition," *Wesleyan Theological Journal* 22, No. 1 (spring 1987): 70.

3. "An Alliance with Sin," *Preacher's Magazine*, July—August 1999, 65.

Chapter 7

1. For an extensive discussion of the various theories, with the advocacy of the penal motif as basic, see my book *God's Integrity and the Cross* (Nappanee, Ind.: Francis Asbury Press of Evangel Publishing House, 1999), 12-20.

2. Geisler, *Chosen but Free*, 85.

3. A. T. Robertson, *Word Pictures in the New Testament*, vol. 4 (New York: Harper and Brothers, Publishers, 1931), 358.

4. David F. Wells interprets the Epistle of 1 John as teaching that "birth from God, which makes us his children, produces true belief in Christ, righteousness of life, and a loving disposition, and makes habitual sin a thing of the past, because sinning is contrary to our renewed moral nature" (*God the Evangelist: How the Holy Spirit Works to Bring Men and Women to Faith* [Grand Rapids: William B. Eerdmans, 1987], 33). Here is a Calvinist who sees clearly the impossibility of living a Christian life while making allowance for willful sin.

Chapter 8

1. Oswald Chambers, *My Utmost for His Highest* (London: Morgan and Scott, 1927), 245.

2. Ibid., 83. Jesse T. Peck, in his classic *The Central Idea of Christianity*, speaks similarly: "Holiness is not an outside or accidental appendage of Christianity. It is the very center of it, the grand element of its power, the essential fact of its value" ([1856; reprint, Salem, Ohio: Schmul Publishing Company, 1999], 111).

3. Literally, the Greek phrase *en hagiasmō pneumatos* means "in or by means of the sanctifying [work] of the Spirit." See 1 Pet. 1:2, where the translation "in the sanctification of the Spirit" (NKJV) is from the identical Greek phrase.

4. This statement implies that Paul was using *amōmos*, blameless, with an intended moral connotation. The flawlessness required of a sacrificial animal in the Old Testament cult becomes here blamelessness of love (not faultlessness of performance). W. E. Vine says that while the Septuagint translators used *amōmos* in reference to unblemished sacrifices required in Leviticus and Numbers, in the Psalms and in Ezekiel it referred to "blamelessness in character and conduct" (*An Expository Dictionary of New Testament Words*, one-vol. ed. [Westwood, N.J.: Fleming H. Revell Company, 1952], 132).

5. H. Ray Dunning takes the position that Pentecost was related to Jesus' prayer in John 17 as God's means of its fulfillment. There Jesus prays that His disciples experience the kind of sanctification that will equip them for the carrying out of their mission. But Dunning says, "That can occur only through a metamorphosis of their nature. Thus the Pentecostal outpouring as well as subsequent ones have as their aim the moral renewal (sanctification) of the disciples so they may carry out this mission. The descriptions of the corporate life of the Early Church validate that Pentecost was clearly effective in accomplishing this result." Speaking of the precise nature of the "promise of the Father" to which Jesus makes reference in Acts 1:4-5, Dunning says this: "The content of Jesus has gone into it, with the result that those who received the Spirit in His fullness understood that not only were they being given a special kind of power to carry on Jesus' mission in the world, but they also were being transformed into a new existence that involved a through-and-through sanctification of their natures" (*Grace, Faith, and Holiness: A Wesleyan Systematic Theology* [Kansas City: Beacon Hill Press of Kansas City, 1988], 422-23).

6. John Wesley, *The Nature of Holiness*, comp. and ed. Clare Weakley Jr. (Minneapolis: Bethany House Publishers, 1988), 77.

7. William M. Greathouse says, "The Spirit of God is the sole explanation of any holiness that we may experience" (*Wholeness in Christ* [Kansas City: Beacon Hill Press of Kansas City, 1999], 129). He quotes Wesley to the same effect: The Holy Spirit is "the immediate cause of all holiness in us." Both Greathouse and Wesley mean the *effectual* cause. The *procuring* cause is Christ, who "loved the church and gave himself up for her to make her holy, and to present her to himself as a radiant church, . . . holy and blameless" (Eph. 5:25-27). (There's that combination of holy and blameless again!)

8. Chambers, *My Utmost for His Highest*, 252.

Chapter 9

1. For an excellent treatment of the place of miracles today, see Wells, *God the Evangelist*, 1987), 79 ff.

2. A. T. Robertson points out that the phrase "and this not from yourselves" refers neither to "faith" nor "grace" but "to the act of being saved by grace conditioned on faith on our part" (*Word Pictures*, vol. 4, 525).

FOR FURTHER READING

Orientation
Carter, Charles W., and Wayne E. Caldwell. *The Genius of the New Testament Church*. Salem, Ohio: Schmul Publishing Company, 1995.

Ingersol, Stan, and Wes Tracy. *Here We Stand*. Kansas City: Beacon Hill Press of Kansas City, 1999.

Lloyd-Jones, D. M. *What Is an Evangelical?* Carlisle, Pa.: Banner of Truth Trust, 1993.

Chapter 1
Comfort, Philip Wesley, ed. *The Origin of the Bible*. Wheaton, Ill.: Tyndale House Publishers, 1992.

Lutzer, Erwin W. *You Can Trust the Bible*. Chicago: Moody Press, 1998.

Taylor, Richard W. *Hearing God's Voice: Biblical Authority and Christian Faith*. Salem, Ohio: Schmul Publishing Co., 2000.

Chapters 2 Through 5
Bloesch, Donald G. *God the Almighty: Power, Wisdom, Holiness, Love*. Downers Grove, Ill.: InterVarsity Press, 1995.

Bray, Gerald. *The Doctrine of God*. Downers Grove, Ill.: InterVarsity Press, 1993.

Lewis, C. S. *The Screwtape Letters* in *The Best of C. S. Lewis*. New York: Iversen Associates, 1969.

Otis, George Jr. *The Twilight Labyrinth: Why Does Spiritual Darkness Linger Where It Does?* Grand Rapids: Chosen Books, 1997.

Chapters 6 Through 9
Collins, Kenneth J. *The Scripture Way of Salvation: The Heart of John Wesley's Theology*. Nashville: Abingdon Press, 1997.

Dayton, Wilber T. *Entire Sanctification: The Divine Purification and Perfection of Man*. Salem, Ohio: Schmul Publishing Company, 2000.

Greathouse, William M. *Wholeness in Christ*. Kansas City: Beacon Hill Press of Kansas City, 1998.

McKenna, David L. *What a Time to Be Wesleyan!* Kansas City: Beacon Hill Press of Kansas City, 1999.

Moore, Frank. *Breaking Free from Sin's Grip*. Kansas City: Beacon Hill Press of Kansas City, 2001.

Rose, Delbert R. *Vital Holiness: A Theology of Christian Experience*. Salem, Ohio: Schmul Publishing Company, 2000.

Tracy, Wes, Gary Cockerill, Donald Demaray, and Steve Harper. *Reflecting God*. Kansas City: Beacon Hill Press of Kansas City, 2000.